Hikes with Tykes

A Practical Guide to Day Hiking with Kids

By Rob Bignell

Atiswinic Press · Ojai, Calif.

HIKES WITH TYKES: *A Practical Guide to Day Hiking with Kids*

Copyright Rob Bignell, 2011
Photographs on pp. 8, 29, 47, 53, 72, 81, 88, 113, 129, 145, 164, 203 by Rob Bignell
Photographs on p. 13, 219 by Cynthia Louise Sharp
Photograph on pp. 35 by Jason Bradshaw
Illustrations on p. 125, 179 by Rob Bignell

All rights reserved. Except for brief passages quoted in newspaper, magazine, radio, television or online reviews, no portion of this book may be reproduced, distributed, or transmitted in any form by any means, electronic or mechanical, including photocopying, recording, or information storage or retrieval system, without the prior written permission of the author.

Atiswinic Press
Ojai, Calif. 93023
http://hikeswithtykes.com/home.html

ISBN 978-0-615-51220-4
Library of Congress Control Number: 2012909505

Cover photos by Rob Bignell

Manufactured in the United States of America
First printing July 2012

For Kieran

ACKNOWLEDGEMENTS

Thank you to all of the parents and colleagues who contributed advice, to Cynthia, Jason and Mary for your photographic skills, and to all who helped proofread.

Contents

INTRODUCTION   *1*

SECTION I: ATTITUDE ADJUSTMENT   *5*

CHAPTER 1: WHY HIKE?   *6*
Bonding · Communing with nature · Exercise · Develop character and skills · Adventure · Establish lifelong activity · These places may not be there when our children are grown · Maintaining your sanity

CHAPTER 2: HIKE LIKE A KID   *12*
Modify your goals · Be flexible · Be patient

CHAPTER 3: PREPARING FOR THE HIKE   *16*
Select a destination · *Great places to hike · When not to hike* · Make a plan · *Planning checklist* · Reluctant little hikers · Inviting others · To camp or not to camp · What to bring

SECTION II: THE RIGHT GEAR   *38*

CHAPTER 4: CLOTHING   *39*
Footwear · Shorts or jeans? · Shirts and jackets · Layering · Headgear · Sunglasses · Rain gear · Winter wear · After the hike

CHAPTER 5: EQUIPMENT   *50*
What you'll need (from baby carriers and backpacks to trekking poles and canteens) · Camping gear · Winter wear · Where to buy gear · *Make your own gear*

CHAPTER 6: NAVIGATIONAL TOOLS   *71*
Paper maps · GPS · Compass · Guidebooks

CHAPTER 7: FOOD AND WATER   *79*
Water · Milk for infants · Food (from snacks to picnic lunches) · Trail mix recipes · What not to bring · Leftovers

CHAPTER 8: SUNDRIES   *87*
Musts (from first aid kit and sunscreen to safety whistles and toilet paper) · Optionals (from binoculars to bathing suits) · Nevers · Sometimes (aka the family dog)

SECTION III: THE HIKE   *101*

CHAPTER 9: ARRIVING AT HIKING AREA   *102*
Packing · *Packing checklist* · Get there sanely · Park safely · Let someone know you've arrived · Secure the vehicle · Emergency information sheet · *Sample emergency information sheet* · *Sample hiker's safety form* · Ready kids for hike · Put on your gear · Go over safety with kids · Locate the trailhead · Who leads?

CHAPTER 10: ON THE TRAIL   *115*
Rules of the trail · Crossing terrain · Trail markers · *Meanings of blazes* · Turn-back time

CONTENTS

CHAPTER 11: NUISANCES *127*
Snail's pace · Running ahead · Potty time · Whining · Boredom · Tantrums · Sibling rivalry · Getting dirty · Noisiness · Risk takers · Reluctant kid · Significant other doesn't enjoy hiking · Fear · Tiredness

CHAPTER 12: ACTIVITIES *139*
Nature-related (from I Spy to identifying tracks) · *Make scavenger hunt cards* · Kid-tested (from Red light, green light to chain story)

SECTION IV: DISASTERS *154*

CHAPTER 13: MEDICAL PROBLEMS *156*
General illnesses · Injuries (from blisters and sunburn to broken bones and unconsciousness)

CHAPTER 14: DANGEROUS PLANTS AND ANIMALS *178*
Troublesome plants (from poison ivy to mushrooms) · *Some poisonous berries* · Animal attacks (from snakes and bug bites to bears and mountain lions)

CHAPTER 15: BAD WEATHER *197*
Lightning · Downpours · Flashfloods · Tornadoes · Snowstorms · Fog

CHAPTER 16: STUCK IN THE WILDS *201*
Forest fires · Lost in the wilds · Forced to stay the night (from building a shelter to starting a campfire)

POSTSCRIPT: AFTER THE HIKE   *218*
Look at your photos · Look at the maps · High point, low point · Share your hike · Get involved · Go back · Save the trail maps

INDEX   *222*

Introduction

> *"If a child is to keep alive his inborn sense of wonder ... he needs the companionship of at least one adult who can share it, rediscovering with him the joy, excitement, and mystery of the world we live in."* – Rachel Carson, *"The Sense of Wonder"*

If you want to change your life – and that of your children – take a hike. Literally.

More importantly, take it together, as parent and child.

Unfortunately, from long-time hikers the suggestion of taking children hiking tends to elicit one of two reactions: They either say it's impossible or they overestimate the abilities of their kids. The first group sadly misses out on a wonderful family experience and gives up a great pastime. The second group creates a hellish experience for themselves and their children and often come to think the first group is right. It is true that with children you'll probably not hike as you did before, but you still can have an enjoyable time on the trails. This book will show you how.

The novice hiker who takes along children always hits the trails with good intent: It's a great way to spend time with the kids, it'll be good exercise, it's something their own parents did with them so a tradition they want to carry on. Unfortunately, novice hikers usually misjudge their abilities and fail to prepare. Especially when kids are involved, that can lead to bad experiences, injury and even death. This book will tell you how to avoid those pitfalls.

"Hikes with Tykes" arises from personal experiences hiking with my son and from those of many other parents who have taken their children on the trail. All of us head into the wilds at least once a week and have been doing so for a long time. I took my son, Kieran, on his first hike when he was but four-months-old, through an old grove of redwood trees that soared 150 feet over our heads. He thoroughly enjoyed it, and we haven't stopped since, peak-bagging mountains, rambling along coastlines, searching fossil and gem trails, and exploring desert canyons, often all in the same month. Now that he's six, we average a couple of day hikes a week.

Each of those hikes has brought us closer together as father and son. We've shared fantastic experiences, from seeing waterfalls off mountain sides to clambering over 20 million-year-old rocks that at one time sat on the ocean floor. We've urged each other up peaks that soar a mile-and-a-half into the sky. We've watched in mutual wonder as tiny bugs carried loads double their weight across roads and as a condor soared above us, its massive wings casting shadows across the bluff walls. All of this was done within a mere 60 miles of our house, on simple trips that took no more than a morning or an afternoon to complete.

This book focuses on such day hikes, the most common way to hit the trails with children until they become teenagers and can carry their own packs deep into the backcountry. Because of that, we won't address camping, rock

INTRODUCTION

climbing, snowshoeing or any of a number of other related outdoor activities. Those topics deserve entire books of their own to be adequately covered.

Day hiking with kids isn't quite as simple as just taking the kids onto a trail and walking. Many parents have no idea where there even is a trail. They wonder how to keep their kids properly dressed for the wilds and how they'll ever carry their infant all those miles. They often struggle with figuring out how much water and food to bring. They know there must be a better way to cross rough terrain than the balancing act they're attempting. They ponder what to do when their children get bored on the trail or start to misbehave. They want to understand how to treat injuries from blisters to broken bones, of what to do if they're lost or even forced to stay the night in the woods. This book will cover that and more.

Kids' safety and comfort is a parental responsibility, and this book provides a number of tips for helping to fulfill that duty. There are a number of long-time, seasoned hikers who immerse their children from birth in the outdoors and a life of adventure, making many of my recommendations in this book sound overcautious. They are extremely experienced hikers, though, and this book is aimed less at them but at the casual hiker and those parents who want to introduce their kids to the outdoors.

Before my son, I usually stuck to walking safe urban parks and sidewalks. Kieran's birth reawakened in me a longing for all of the grand adventures I had as a child, when I grew up on a farm and days were spent wandering about the fields and nearby woods. I wanted to share those experiences with him. Living in Northern California near

Redwood National Park, I decided to explore the same backcountry trails as the tourists who visited our town. Hiking into the backcountry was an entirely different experience from walking the hay rows as a kid with a branch in my hand, though. Learning how to backpack was easy enough – there were plenty of books on it, and I'd served in the infantry – but adding a child to the mix was something I had to largely figure out on my own. Some hiking books mention special considerations that should be made for children but usually in a cursory manner. As talking to my parenting friends scattered across the country who also hiked, they told of experiencing the same trials and tribulations as me.

On the pages ahead, I want to share what we've learned and in doing so hope you and your kids will come to love hiking as much as Kieran and I.

Section I: Attitude Adjustment

"In every walk with nature one receives far more than he seeks." - John Muir

Maybe you're tired of playing tea party or of hearing the *blip-blip-zap!* of the videogame DeathRaid 3000 for what feels like the millionth time. Maybe you used to hike into the backcountry before the kids came along. Maybe you've always wondered where that trail leading into unknown, which you see from the road everyday on your way to work, actually goes. Whatever the reason, you've decided to go hiking.

That's a good thing, for both you and your children.

But don't harbor any notions of hiking 14 miles deep into the backcountry and spending a night in the wilds. At least not at first. Maybe after many, many far shorter hikes and when the kids are older that will be possible. But not now.

In this section, we'll examine some basic principles you should follow when day hiking with children and then go into detail about how to select the right trail for you and your children. First, though, let's discuss why you should take your children hiking, just in case you're still harboring a few doubts about the whole enterprise.

Chapter 1: Why Hike?

Listing excuses of why not to hike with children is easy enough: Kids wouldn't enjoy it, I don't know where there's a trail, it takes too much time, I'm out of shape, it's too expensive.

All of those arguments are fallacies. Kids generally love to be outdoors. There's probably a hiking trail within a few miles of your house, even if you live in the middle of a major metro area. Hiking these trails often only takes a couple of hours or at most an afternoon. Walking a day hiking trail is a good way to get back into shape. Hiking also is very inexpensive, requiring very little gear or clothing that isn't already in the closet and not requiring any hotels or restaurants. You generally don't need to pay entry fees (and when you do they're typically low), and usually there's no place where a child can demand you buy toys.

More than likely, the real reasons you're not hiking is because planning for a trip can be intimidating, and as a parent you have real fears for your children's safety. This book will guide you through the planning process and giving you the knowledge to ensure you and your children remain safe. After all, both you and your children will benefit in a number of ways from hiking.

Bonding

This is the main reason to take your kids hiking: to spend quality time with your children. The trail marks a place where you can grow closer together, where unhindered by the distractions of mobile phone texts, emails and the next television program we can talk with one another, where you can revel together in discovery.

Hiking with young children can lead to a family tradition, experiences that later in life both parent and full-grown child will reminisce fondly about.

Communing with nature

As adults, we need the natural world because we are incomplete without it. Kids, too, need to get away from the pressures and hectic pace of modern life. Kids these days lead structured lives of schoolwork, soccer practices, music lessons and more; they need an opportunity to escape it with the ones they love, their family members. Nature can help them relax and relieve stress. The sights of the natural world can raise our spirits, can inspire us as we enjoy refuge from the modern world.

Being a very small creature in the wilds or as looking upon some fantastic vista can put your whole life in a broader perspective.

Rambling and exploring in nature can enrich children's lives. Too many kids suffer from what many hikers and others who appreciate the great outdoors call "nature-deficit disorder." Experiencing nature is an extremely important part of growing up and maturing, argues Richard Louv in "Last Child in the Woods: Saving Our Children from Nature-Deficit Disorder," as it inspires imaginative and creative play. Indeed, going into the wilds is like wandering through a living museum, and for some urban kids akin to visiting an alien world.

Almost everything in the natural world intrigues children, making a hike the perfect adventure.

Hiking also can enrich our lives as adults. Kids notice things in nature that we adults have long taken for granted. A child can reawaken our wonderment of and appreciation for the natural world.

The trail is where children learn to enjoy, respect and love nature. Hearing the varied sounds of birds and feeling against one's cheek the splash of a waterfall builds the compassion that raises our children to become stewards of the natural world. The earlier we expose children to the outdoors, the more they'll take to it.

Exercise

Hiking is a low impact exercise that's invigorating. It helps strengthen muscles, the heart and lungs, builds stamina and endurance. Walking certainly is necessary, especially at a time of high obesity in the United States – but why limit yourself to walking alone on a treadmill inside a building when you could be with your family breathing in fresh mountain air or feeling the breeze off an ocean through your hair? The faster you go on the trail adds an aerobic element to the workout, allowing you to tone muscle.

Kids have a lot of energy. Give them an interesting place where they can run it off, and you've made for a fun day. At the very least, running around in the fresh air is a guaranteed good night's sleep.

Develop character and skills

On the trail, children can learn patience, goal setting, self-sufficiency and self-confidence, all while increasing their attention spans, so challenged these days by fast-moving, action-packed television programs and video games. The physical challenge of the journey and of reaching a summit or an incredible destination generates a supreme sense of achievement in adult and child alike.

Hiking encourages creative, imaginative play. The television set and today's video games are largely passive activities – the story is told for you, and you don't have to think much if at all. Being in nature, however, requires you to interact in deeper ways with the world around you.

That's not all, though. Depending on the activities you do together on the trail, children can improve their language and even their math skills without ever doing a worksheet or cracking a textbook. They can learn about man's interplay with the natural world by observing first-hand dams, clear cutting and mining.

Adventure

In the wilds, children will feel wonderment, going places they cannot see any other way. Discovery, exploring the unknown, testing themselves, just having plain old fun … it's a real adventure, which is infinitely more satisfying than the virtual one they would experience on the couch.

Establish lifelong activity

Kids exposed to the outdoors at an early age usually love the outdoors through their lives. Hiking can be a fun, healthy, safe, social activity that they enjoy during their trying teen years. As they enter adulthood, their love of the trail can lead to mastering other outdoor activities, such as rock climbing, trail running, mountaineering, caving, canoeing, fishing, kayaking, skiing, snowshoeing, ice climbing and more.

These places may not be there when our children are grown

Continued urbanization, overuse by an expanding population, and climate change all likely mean many wilderness spots will look quite different in a quarter century. Even though most of the places you'll hike are protected, human activity certainly will change them.

That was never so clear to Mike C. of Los Angeles than after the 2009 Station Fire, which destroyed nearly half of the Angeles National Forest:

> *"My son and I had spent the entire summer hiking its trails, from pine-covered mountain-*

tops to desert canyons, from trails that overlook the entire L.A. sprawl to remote fire lookout towers. For some reason, I always thought the forest would remain like that forever. In a few short days, a fire swept over every trail we walked that summer, leaving it all a barren, ash-covered wasteland. It'll take 60 years for the forest to look again like that summer we hiked it."

Maintaining your sanity

If you are a hiker, you don't have to give up your pastime just because of children. You may not be able to go as far or as high as you would like for some time, but you still can hit the trails and do something that is just as satisfying: teaching a young child to love the wilds as well. If you've never really hiked before, getting outside and discovering new sights with the kids marks a great way to break the indoors doldrums and stifling routines of everyday life.

Regardless if a hiker or not, we can learn from our children by rediscovering nature through their eyes. They see the world from a different perspective – not just with the innocent eyes of youth but by being so much smaller than we are. They literally look at the world from different angles than we do.

Chapter 2: Hike like a Kid

To enjoy hiking with kids, you'll first have to adopt your child's perspective. Simply put, we must learn to hike on our kids' schedules – even though they may not know that's what we're doing.

Modify your goals

Compared to adults, kids can't walk as far, they can't walk as fast, and they will grow bored more quickly. Every step we take requires three for them. In addition, early walkers, up to 2 years of age, prefer to wander than to "hike." Preschool kids will start to walk the trail, but at a rate of only about a mile per hour. With stops, that can turn a three-mile hike into a four-hour journey. Kids also won't be able to hike as steep of trails as you or handle as inclement of weather as you might.

This all may sound limiting, especially to long-time backpackers used to racking up miles or bagging peaks on their hikes, but it's really not. While you may have to put off some backcountry and mountain climbing trips for a while, it also opens up to you a number of great short trails and nature hikes with spectacular sights that you may have otherwise skipped because they weren't challenging enough.

So sure, you'll have to make some compromises … but the payout is high. You're not personally on the hike to get

Children often will want to stop and explore or just enjoy the scenery, forcing adults to reappraise their hiking goals.

a workout but to spend quality time with your children. And they'll always get older and be able to go farther.

Be careful, though, what you wish for. With older teenagers, the problem becomes quite the opposite of toddlers – keeping up with their high metabolism.

Be flexible

When hiking with children, you may need to rest longer than you planned. You may need to eat lunch earlier or later than planned. You may find kids aren't interested in seeing what you think is exciting but instead are entirely taken in by something else that utterly bores you.

You may never reach the end of the trail. But that's all right; "bailing" is okay. When hiking with kids, the point is the journey, not the destination.

Be patient

Children will explore and touch everything on the way. In contrast, most adults hike with the goal of reaching a destination as quickly as they can, as accomplishment of a goal or seeing something spectacular at the endpoint shapes their perception of what a hike should be. To the child, the journey itself is exciting, and much of what is seen along the way is new and intriguing. What may be mundane to adults may mark the first time a child has ever encountered a bird pecking against a tree, a bug crossing a trail, or a frog sitting on a lily pad. Let them stand in the hollow tree or peak their head into a dark cave.

Kids will want to engage their senses. Let them get a little dirty and touch the squishy mud, rub their hands against the rough bark, or stick their nose into the wildflower. Just make sure they don't touch dangerous plants, like poison ivy.

As Laurence K. of Boulder, Colo., advises:

> *"Don't turn the hike a death march. For younger children, the experience, not the accomplish-*

ment, is what matters. As children enter their teen years and close on adulthood, they'll start thinking more and more about achieving goals on the trail."

In addition, don't correct everything your kid does wrong, instead, praise. For every correction made, praise for three things done right; if kid connects hiking with parent criticism, they'll quickly come to dislike hiking.

While we're not doing an adult hike, anymore, we do remain parents, and as such we must remain alert at all times. Hiking can be dangerous, but only when we fail to be safe.

Chapter 3: Preparing for the Hike

You'll get more out of the hike if you research it and plan ahead. It's not enough to just pull over to the side of the road and hit a trail that you've never been on and have no idea where it goes. In fact, doing so invites disaster.

When selecting a destination, remember that not all kids are made alike. The five-year-old neighbor boy may have had no trouble with a specific trail, but your five-year-old may not like it or be able to handle it. There's nothing wrong with that. We're all different and develop at our own rates.

Select a destination

The best advice when choosing a trail is to "do your homework." There's a lot to consider, from its length to elevation gains, from weather to what features you'll see on the trail.

For your first few hikes, stick to short, well-known trails where you're likely to encounter others. Once you get a feel for hiking and your kids' abilities and interests, expand to longer and more remote trails.

Until they enter their late teens, children need to stick to trails rather than going off-trail hiking, which is known as bushwhacking. Children too easily can get lost when off

PREPARING FOR THE HIKE

trail. They also can easily get scratched and cut up or stumble across poisonous plants and dangerous animals.

Finding out about trails

How do you know where there's a trail to hike? Maybe you may live near a park or national forest and pass a trail on your way to work or when running errands. You may have overheard other hikers or parents talking about them. Even then, you probably don't know much about those trails or if they're right for you and your family.

You may not be so lucky, of course, and have no idea where you can even hike. To find the answer, go online and look for trails near you, simply by entering the name of your town and "hiking trails" in a search engine. You may need to enter the state along with your town – for example, just typing "Lancaster" for your town gives you results for both the city in California and the one in Pennsylvania. Many of the websites you encounter will be blogs, discussion boards, and chat rooms about hiking. They can give you insights on what to expect on the trail and problems encountered.

Alternatively, you might look on a map and see what parks or national forests are near you (See the special section in this chapter on "Great Places to Hike" for the upsides and pitfalls of differing parks.).

Most guidebooks tend to list trails that offer the most dramatic views or that are the most famous among adult hikers. You'll have to be selective to find those that work well for a child. Usually those marked "easy" are good trails to consider.

Great Places to Hike

There are some ideal places to start your search for a great hiking trail – and some places you'll want to avoid.

Green light, go!

National and state parks
- National parks typically boast the region's most stunning sights. Unfortunately, they can be crowded, and unless you live right next to one, it's going to be a long drive. That may be fine for teenagers but may not be worth it for younger kids when you'll spend more time on the road than the trail. In addition, long drives probably mean you'll be staying overnight, often an expensive proposition.
- If living near a national park or traveling cross country, by all means stop and hike through it. There will be a great variety of trails to choose from, and the scenery will make them highly memorable.
- You'll also need to pay an entry fee for national parks. If you plan to hike national parks regularly, you should consider purchasing a National Parks and Federal Recreational Lands Pass, which will get a noncommercial vehicle plus passholder and three passengers into any national park for less than $100 a year. Even less expensive versions of the pass are available for senior citizens, the disabled and National Park volunteers.
- State parks sometimes are a little less scenic than national parks but still offer a variety of beautiful sights and a great adventure for kids. They're also a lot closer than most national parks, meaning shorter drives and little need to stay overnight. You usually will have to pay a fee to enter or park your vehicle.

PREPARING FOR THE HIKE

National forests
- Run by the U.S. Forest Service, national forests are more numerous and therefore probably closer to you than national parks. The quality of the trails vary greatly within national forests, and be forewarned: often public facilities are lacking.
- Generally, you will need a pass to use the trails. You can buy annual or daily passes; if you plan to do more than a half-dozen hikes a year in a national forest, the annual Adventure Pass is the best deal. Also, be aware that the pass isn't for all national forests but just a group of them. You may need to buy additional passes if heading into a forest not covered by yours.

County parks
- Most county parks are rural in nature, so there's often a forest component to them. You also can find a number of short trails in many county parks.
- While they don't offer the majestic arches and mile-deep canyons of national parks, they are scenic in their own right and usually only a few miles drive from where you live.
- An added benefit is that most county parks are free unless you intend to camp.

Beaches
- Don't just think Southern California, Florida and Hawaii. The United States has a colossal number of beachfronts up and down the Atlantic seaboard, the Pacific Ocean, the Gulf of Mexico and the Great Lakes, as well as numerous inland lakes, ponds and rivers.
- If you're looking on a map for a place to hike, just spy a blue line, and you're sure to find along it a municipal, county or state park that boasts great trails and views.

Gem and fossil trails

- Some trails will take you and your children to great locations where they easily can find gems or even fossils. This is a great way to get kids interested in rockhounding and to teach them about geology.
- Collecting can be an issue as some sites on national and state land prohibit the removal of rocks and fossils, so always check the regulations. It's no fun for a kid to go find beautiful agates or 20-million-year-old fossilized palm fronds only to have to leave them behind.
- If heading down a gem or fossil trail, you'll need a geologist's hammer, goggles to protect your eyes when you start digging, and re-sealable plastic bags to carry the collected rocks.

BLM land

- The Bureau of Land management, an agency of the U.S. Department of the Interior, looks after public lands. About an eighth of the nation – more than 260 million acres – are public lands managed by the BLM, and you can go on most of it anytime you like. That's a lot of land to hike, and if you live in the West, it's probably not far from your city limits.

National Natural Landmarks

- Nearly 600 locations across the country have been named landmarks for the geological and ecological uniqueness in a National Park Service program. They range from volcanic calderas to caves.
- Though lacking the amenities of a national park, many of these areas are magnificent sites that few people visit or even know about. Hiking trails run through many of them. They're also all free.

PREPARING FOR THE HIKE

Yellow light, slow!

Wildlife sanctuaries and refuges

■ Some wildlife sanctuaries and nature reserves have hiking trails to enjoy, but a number of them would prefer that humans not encroach on the area. It is, after all, an area set aside for wildlife, usually those that are endangered. Check with the organization that oversees the sanctuary you're interested in entering.

■ Those reserves that do have trails open to the public are great places to spot wildlife, particularly birds. Given this, the best times to hike them may be during very specific times of the year.

Red light, stop!

Private property

■ Always ask permission before going on someone's land. Respect "No Trespassing" signs.

■ Unless you're asking a neighbor you know because you want to stay close to home during a walk, there really is no need to hike private property. Public trails abound.

Hiking or camping magazines also offer lists, but they tend to be for serious backpackers who go long distances on multi-day trips.

Organized hikes offered at local parks also are a great way to get started. The downside is they often move slow and don't always stop and linger where your child might want to.

If you can't find answers about a specific trail, additional information usually can be obtained from park rangers.

Factors in selecting the right trail

Once you've got a few trails in mind for hiking, you'll need to decide if they're right for you and your children. Remember that because children are involved, your choices naturally will be more restrictive than if selecting one for yourself or for adults alone to walk.

Local weather and seasons

Always check to see what the weather will be like on the trail you plan to hike. While an adult might be able to withstand wind and a sprinkle here or there, for children it can be pure misery. Dry, pleasantly warm days with limited wind always are best when hiking with children. That eliminates some climates during specific seasons; deserts, for example, are verboten in summer as are high mountains in winter.

The age of your child also matters. Generally, older teens will be able to handle inclement weather better that younger children. Cold weather is a no-no for infants.

That being said, hiking in winter is quite popular in Northern states and mountain areas where outdoor activities are common year around. Not being able to hike in winter would limit the activity to a few months out of the year. Winter hiking has its advantages, as well, such as no bugs and smaller (and often no) crowds. It also is more of a challenge.

Consider what the trail will be like as well. If it's open, as would be one in the desert or a meadow, you can expect a lot of sun and probably wind. The sunshine may be just fine on cooler days. During the hot days of summer, though, look for tree-lined, shaded trails.

PREPARING FOR THE HIKE

When Not to Hike

As selecting a trail, you can eliminate those in certain regions when specific weather conditions prevail:

■ **Coastlines** – Always check local tide tables if walking along beaches and coastlines, as you don't want to get stranded in the ocean or large lake by rising water.

■ **Cold climates** – Winter and spring will be chilly and often wet.

■ **Deserts** – Avoid them during the wet seasons as flash floods can occur, sweeping down sandy washes and canyons, leaving you stranded, wet, or worse drowned. Outside of the wet season, avoid any days in which rain, high wind, and hot temperatures are forecast. This makes summer a bad time for desert hiking. Late autumn and early spring usually are the best times to hike deserts.

■ **Forests** – Spring usually is a wet season to avoid. Summer and autumn make for the best hiking.

■ **High altitudes** – Whenever high winds, precipitation and cold temperatures are forecast at lower elevations, they will be worse in the mountains. Winter, early spring and late autumn are dangerous times to hike high mountains. Low mountains and hilly country are best hiked on pleasant spring days; late summer is best for high mountains.

In addition, check to see if the area you intend to hike is in high tourist season or if a local festival is going on nearby. Both usually occur during dry, pleasantly warm weather – which coincidentally are the best days for hiking with children. Such events can result in busy trails and heavy traffic.

[23]

HIKES WITH TYKES

One high tourist season you probably won't be able to avoid is flower and foliage displays, though. Often the main reason to go to some parks is for their wildflower displays.

Also, don't hike during high hunting seasons. There's really no sane reason, for example, to hit a Wisconsin trail during Thanksgiving week's deer hunting season, when more than 225,000 armed hunters with buck fever comb virtually every woods and field.

Knowing the weather also can result in a lighter load. There's very little need to bring wet weather gear if there's no rain forecast for a 100 miles around and you're going to be out for just a couple of hours. If on a hike of more than a couple of hours, though, be aware that weather fronts can move quickly, turning a lovely sunny morning into a bitterly cold, gray afternoon.

Weather forecasting is a difficult craft at best. A prediction about temperatures and rainfall usually is only good for about 48 hours. Though you may have planned the weekend hike Wednesday evening, canceling the hike on a gray Saturday morning always is better than spending a few extra days in the wilds hoping a rescue team finds you because you were cut off high waters.

Distance/length

Don't choose a trail that is any longer than the youngest child in your group can hike. Adults in good shape can go 8-12 miles a day; for kids, it's much less.

There's no magical number. Ask other parents what their children can do, and you'll get a whole range of answers. The reality is that every child is different: different

PREPARING FOR THE HIKE

leg lengths, different attitudes toward hiking, different levels of physical fitness, different levels of physical development, different expectations about being carried, and more.

Here's what some parents recommend:

> "A general rule of thumb: A physically fit child of three can handle a flat nature trail of about a mile. When children turn five, they probably can go longer distances, certainly no more than 5 miles if the terrain is flat, but they'll be able to handle shorter distances with small elevation gains. Ten-year-olds can start to handle steep climbs of up to a couple of miles. Five-mile hikes are the maximum for a fit teenager, presuming they are carrying a backpack. A motivated and energetic child easily could do more than these guidelines recommend – and a physically fit child who is tired and bored likely will do less." – Kristen Y., Jackson, Wyo.

> "A half a mile for every year of age is about right, so a four-year-old could go two miles, a six-year-old can go three miles, and so on." – Richard I., Flagstaff, Ariz.

> "I've often heard the half-mile per year rule. That probably works for a motivated child walking on a rather flat surface, but I find the numbers a bit high. A 14-year-old on a seven-mile hike? That was tough in the Army when I was 18!" – Wes L., Juneau, Alaska

The moral of the story is you'll have to gauge what your children can and are willing to do. By starting with short hikes, you'll learn your children's limits and then can build up to longer walks. Indeed, if you start them young and make it fun, most kids soon will want to go on long hikes.

Whatever you do, don't think too big. The farther you plan to go and the higher you plan to climb, the bigger the disappointment will be for you when you don't make it – and the more discouraged the children will be, too. The more ambitious your first few hikes, the greater the likelihood that all of you will sour on hiking.

Another element to consider is how far you can carry a child. Parent hikers often take their infants and toddlers with them in baby carriers, but there's only so far you can walk with a little one on your hip or back. In addition, if you exceed a walking child's limitations, you'll end up carrying them or their gear out. Should a child be injured, you may have to carry them as well. So know your limitations.

As determining a trail's length, remember that a map is a 2D representation of the terrain. Adding up miles on a map doesn't equal the true over-the-ground distance. When driving, a mile or two may not make a difference, but walking an extra mile or three can be a nightmare for a child. Fortunately, most guidebooks and websites list a trail's actual walking miles, but if you can't find that info, keep in mind that a map can be deceptive.

You don't have to hike the entire trail, of course. Many times I've just hiked to an interesting geographical feature that was a mile or two up the trail then turned around and

PREPARING FOR THE HIKE

headed home. So go ahead and look at long trails to see if there is anything interesting on the way in.

Just don't have your heart set on reaching the trail's endpoint.

Elevation gains

"The perfect trail goes downhill both ways." – Dianne J., Seattle

For teenagers, peakbagging or hiking to a mountain's summit, can be fun. The younger the child, though, and you'll want to avoid switchbacks and large elevation gains. Simply put, the younger the flatter. A single high knoll can wear out a three-year-old kid who otherwise could handle a mile of flat ground. If the child is walking, limit elevation gains to 500 feet for older elementary school children and to even less for preschoolers.

Quality of trail

There are three elements to consider about the trail's quality:

- **Turf** – If the trail surface is extremely rocky or sandy, children will have difficulty walking across them. Maintaining your footing on rocks is difficult, and feet tend to sink in sand. This is not to say a trail ought to be void of rocks and sand, but it shouldn't consist entirely of them where young kids are concerned. A smooth trail is best.

- **Width** – Trails that are too wide or too narrow can pose problems. A wide path, such as one larger than a single lane road, removes kids too much from nature and tends to leave them exposed to sunlight. A narrow path not any wider than your body often means children are going to rub up against bushes and tree branches, potentially resulting in scratches and ticks. A trail that is a little wider than an adult body and no more than a single lane of road (known as a jeep trail) usually is best.

■ **Overgrown** – When plants block portions of the trail and prevent you from seeing where you are going, the path has become overgrown and is in need of maintenance. Young children are certain to be scratched and cut on such a trail. Stepping through the overgrowth also is a good way to surprise animals, some potentially dangerous, such as snakes.

Uniqueness

A hike of quiet reflection through the woods may sound great for an adult, but it's a big bore to kids. They want to see things along the way – lakes and ponds, interesting rock formations, waterfalls, fire lookout towers, wildflowers, streams, boulder fields, sweeping vistas, nature center, abandoned buildings (though you won't go in them), fossils, stream crossings (only for older kids) and more. Water almost always is a winner with kids.

A trail with an intriguing history probably won't mean much to kids until they're at least in their late elementary school years. The concept of history is too abstract for most young children, who have a limited notion of time spanning a day let alone years.

When planning the hike, try to find a trail that has a midpoint payoff – that is something kids will find exciting about half-way through the hike. This will help keep kids' energy and enthusiasm up during the journey.

PREPARING FOR THE HIKE

When planning a hike with children, look for an interesting destination or midpoint payoff, like a fire lookout tower.

Generally, kids will prefer a circular route to one that requires hiking back the way you came. The return trip on an out-and-back trail often feels anti-climatic, but you can overcome that by mentioning features that all of you might want to take a closer look at.

Dangers

It's good to know what plants and animals are in the area you'll be hiking, so you can avoid them. If you don't know much about the plants or animals – such as what they look like – you'll want to research that, too:

> *"We took a hike in northern Vermont during the fall when the foliage was a blaze of colors. I guess I was a little too taken in because I didn't pay attention to what the trees were telling me: We were walking into bear country. The trail wound through beechnut, apple, and cherry, all of which produced fruits that bears gorge on as they near hibernation. When we spotted a big sow just off the trail, we froze. Luckily we were downwind from it and were able to turn back with incident."* – Vera E., Burlington, Vt.

How far of a drive?

The younger the child, the shorter the distance from home you want the trail to be. When my Kieran was two-years-old, more than a half-hour in the Jeep to the trailhead was murder – even with toys and books and his favorite stuffie. As a four-year-old, he could handle a trip of up to an hour. You probably already have a good idea of how long your children can spend in the vehicle.

There are a couple of other elements to consider about the drive. Even if your children have no problem with two or three hours in the car, long drives can cramp muscles. For infants, curvy roads like those in the mountains can lead to upset tummies. Neither situation will make for a pleasant hike.

Timing the hike

How long will the entire adventure take? To determine that, add three elements: drive time, walking time, and rest stops. Drive time usually is easy to figure out, though be aware that if heading into mountains, curvy and steep roads will force you to go slower. That means a longer drive time. For walking time, you'll go much slower than you would if hiking on your own or with other adults. Kids on your back probably will increase your walk time by 25%; kids on foot will increase it by 50% until their late teens, when they'll probably outpace you. Finally, set aside 10-15 minutes for each rest stop on the hike, stopping every half hour for toddlers, preschoolers and early elementary school aged-children and every hour for older children and teens. Of course, you may need to make more frequent stops, but don't do any less.

This hike now must be positioned during certain hours of the day depending on your children's habits. Most importantly, consider when your kids eat meals and take naps. You're trying to squeeze hikes between these major daily events in a child's life.

For infants, this is not such a big deal as the child can be fed during rest stops, and the rhythm of your walk likely will lull him to sleep. For toddlers eating solid meals and needing the comfort of a mattress, however, it's a bit more complicated. You don't want to arrive at the trailhead a half-hour before lunch time. This all becomes less of an issue as the children enter school; if the hike crosses meal time, simply plan a picnic lunch. Regardless of age, make sure kids have eaten a complete meal before heading out on the road.

You also want to get back to you vehicle before darkness falls. Children hiking at night is inadvisable, as the difficulty in seeing increases the chance of falling, of missing a turnoff in the trail and getting lost, and of keeping track of them. Many animals also hunt at night, so there is a greater chance of being bitten.

That being said, group night hikes, led by rangers and park docents, are a lot of fun and very educational – but the trails on such hikes usually are wide and well maintained, and you're probably with a highly experienced hiker who knows the area extremely well.

Ensure trail isn't closed

Sometimes trails are closed for maintenance or because fires and landslides have made them impassable. As you research trails online to determine their length, terrain and features, watch for information that indicates whether or not the trail is closed. To be certain, contact the ranger for the park, forest or wilderness area you plan to visit.

Make a plan

Once you select a trail, map out your route. Using a light, transparent highlighter that won't obscure details, trace the trail on your map. This will make navigating the path easier once in the field.

Make sure you pack the maps with your gear, and tell someone where you are going and when you plan to return.

Also, know where the nearest hospital or walk-in clinic is located. If an injury occurs, you may need to bring your children there for medical help.

PREPARING FOR THE HIKE

Planning checklist

Before leaving on any hike, plan out your trip:

■ Print a road map showing how to reach the parking lot near the trailhead. Outline the route with a transparent yellow highlighter and write out the directions.
■ Print a satellite photo of the parking area and the trailhead. Mark the trailhead on the photo.
■ Print a topo map of the trail. Outline the trail with the yellow highlighter. Note interesting features you want to see along the trail and the destination.
■ If carrying GPS, program this information into your device.
■ Make a timeline for your trip, listing: when you will leave home; when you will arrive at the trailhead; your turn-back time (see Chapter 10); when you will return for home in your vehicle; when you will arrive at home.
■ Estimate how much water and food you will need to bring based on the amount of time you plan to spend on the trail and in your vehicle. You'll need at least 2 pints of water per person for every hour on the trail.
■ Fill out two copies of a hiker's safety form (see sample in Chapter 9). Leave one in your vehicle.
■ Share all of this information with a responsible person remaining in civilization, leaving a hiker's safety form with them. If they do not hear from you within an hour of when you plan to leave the trail in your vehicle, they should contact authorities to report you as possibly lost.

You'll want to do your research a couple of days before hitting the trail. Give yourself an hour or two to look up and sift through the information. Sometimes you'll be lucky and find all you need to know about a trail in a guidebook or at a hiking blog post. More often than not, you'll want to do research beyond that information, and that can take time. It also can be quite fun, as you'll soon find yourself getting energized about hiking the trail!

Reluctant little hikers
Kids can be fickle creatures. Their lack of knowledge and experience in the world often makes them cautious about suggested activities.

You want to sway kids to at least entertain the notion that a hike might be fun. If they hit the trail thinking a long stretch of boredom awaits them, they'll make the experience miserable for both themselves and for you.

To entice kids, let them help plan the hike. They can help select the destination, trace out the trail on a map, choose which snacks to bring, and so on.

For younger kids, find coloring pages about hiking on the Internet that you can print for free (just type "hiking coloring pages" in a search engine for images). Coloring pages showing children having fun and some of the scenery on the trail often gets kids excited about the adventure ahead.

Show them pictures of interesting animals, plants and rock formations they might see on the trail. Photos taken by other hikers of a trail usually can be found online. Remember, though, that flowers are seasonal and most animals prefer not to be seen, so some of the photos you'll find may not represent what you'll actually observe along the trail when you plan to hike it.

PREPARING FOR THE HIKE

Kids who get to carry their own daypack – just like the adults – often will readily go on a hike.

You also can get a library book about hiking, showing all of the fun that can be had on such an adventure. If your library uses the Dewey Decimal System (and most do), you can find hiking books aimed at kids in the 796s of the juvenile nonfiction section. If hitting a gem or fossil trail, pick up a book about rockhounding in the 552s.

Children also can make their own hiking gear. Trekking poles and a utility belt to hold a water bottle and snacks don't have to be purchased but can be constructed using materials you probably have in the yard or garage. Read more on this in Chapter 5.

Finally, don't call it a "hike." Some kids think a "hike" means a death march through boring countryside. Instead, you are going on an "adventure," an "expedition" or a "trek" – or say "we're going to see a waterfall at the end of a trail." For really hard to crack nuts say, "We're walking to a pool where we'll swim." Now you're not hiking but swimming, from the child's point of view. Also, express your own wonderment and enthusiasm about nature. For younger children, it soon will be infectious.

Inviting others

If your children are older, allowing a friend to come along is a great way to keep them excited about the trip. With younger children, though, this primarily is your time to bond with them.

Bringing another adult can be invaluable in helping during an emergency or assisting in carrying the load. On the downside, you could end up spending more time talking to the other adult than interacting with your kids. With older children, that may not be an issue, but with preschoolers and early elementary school kids, it may send the message that they are unimportant – then again, they may be just too busy exploring all the natural world has to offer to even notice. You'll have to decide what's right for you and your child.

To camp or not to camp?

Often hiking is done in conjunction with camping. Discomfort, lack of modern facilities, and being away from toys for a long time makes camping a bad idea for some children. For others, it's a great adventure. You know your child best and will have to determine if camping is right for your family. As the scope of this book is day hiking with children, the advice in this book presumes you won't be camping, which greatly decreases the amount and type of gear and supplies you'll have to carry.

What to bring

Knowing the answers to the questions that go into determining where you'll hike – weather, trail conditions, features you'll see there – will help you determine what kind of clothing and gear to bring. The age of your children also will play a significant role in making these decisions.

Generally, you want to go as light as possible. The more you carry, the heavier the load and so the greater the physical exertion. A lighter load also decreases the chance of injury and means you can go farther. In addition, the more you bring, the odds increase that you'll lose or forget something.

During the next few chapters, we'll discuss some of the clothing and gear you'll need.

Section II: The Right Gear

Getting the right gear – from clothing to equipment such as backpacks and canteens, from snacks to first-aid items such as adhesive bandages and tweezers – is vital. Don't expect a kid to tough it out on the trail. A few might, but most won't because they simply can't. Children aren't fully developed physically or mentally, and so we must make special considerations for their needs on the trail. In this section, we'll examine how to best outfit your children and you for a successful day hike.

Chapter 4: Clothing

When my son and I lived in Southern California where the weather usually is pleasantly warm and dry, a T-shirt with shorts, hiking boots and hiking socks was about all that my son and I donned for the wilderness. Sometimes during the cooler months, we might opt for jeans instead of shorts and pull on a sweatshirt. During the summer months, a hat with a brim was mandatory. It was that simple.

But that's Southern California where checking the weather usually is as uncomplicated as looking out the window. In contrast, Midwestern states are notorious for having four seasons in a single day. The chances of hiking a sunny day in the Pacific Northwest are less than the chances of getting wet. In Florida, an afternoon shower is a daily occurrence during the summer. Most locales demand that you dress differently for each hike, even one done a few days before. In any case, you'll need some special clothing, like footwear and socks. Not having them greatly increases your chance of injury.

When buying hiking clothes, remember that this pastime isn't about being fashionable or wearing the most expensive duds. It's about being comfortable and protecting yourself from the elements.

Fortunately, a variety of practical, functional and good looking clothing is available in all price ranges.

Footwear

If a child's feet hurt, the hike is over, so getting the right footwear is worth the time.

Making sure the footwear fits before hitting the trail also is worth it. If you've gone a few weeks without hiking, that's plenty of time for your children to grow, and they may have just outgrown their hiking boots. Check out their footwear a few days before heading out on the hike. If it doesn't fit, replace it.

Shoes and boots

For flat, smooth, dry trails, sneakers and cross-trainers are just fine; but if you really want to head onto less traveled roads or tackle areas that aren't typically dry (like Southern California is), you'll need hiking boots.

Once you start doing any rocky or steep trails – and remember that a trail you consider moderately steep needs to be only half that angle for a child to consider it extremely steep – you'll want hiking boots, which offer rugged tread perfect for handling rough trails.

Also, in some parts of the nation, such as the Pacific Northwest, parts of the trails will be muddy even after a few days of dry weather have passed. Sneakers quickly will become soaked and unable to traverse mud.

Hiking boots don't just give you traction. If your children don't have good shoes, they run the risk of blisters or even punctures from sharp rocks.

Adults also should wear hiking boots, as they have either a baby carrier or a backpack strapped over their shoulders. If lugging about nothing more than a small

CLOTHING

daypack, you probably can get away with wearing cross-trainers, trekking shoes or trail-running shoes so long as you stick to fairly level, short footpaths.

Shop for hiking boots in the afternoon when feet are slightly swollen from having been walked on earlier that day. Also wear the socks you plan to don when hiking. If you wear insoles or orthotics, make sure they go into the boot as well.

The smaller the child, aim for lightweight shoes. Five-pound shoes would be cumbersome for most adults, so imagine what they would be for a child with smaller, less muscular legs. Indeed, an old hikers' axiom is that a pound of shoe weight equals five pounds in the backpack.

Look for the following in a hiking boot:

■ **Fit** – Ill-fitting boots means blisters and foot pain. A boot should feel snug, yet you should be able to wriggle toes and have no pressure points. Some parents purchase a boot one shoe size too big for the child so that it can accommodate the thicker socks that hiking requires.

■ **Support** – A good boot for day hiking will have a soft collar to support the ankle and to keep pebbles or other debris from getting into the shoe. Ankle-high boots will give good support without restricting movement. Velcro straps are fine for toddlers, but older children will benefit from laces as they help reduce slippage. If the boot allows your foot to flatten out, then it's not providing enough arch support.

■ **Sturdy** – The sole and the boot's upper part should be firmly attached. It ought to be flexible enough that you have a full range of motion but not at the price of the boot stressing so it can't provide support.

- **Water-resistant** – A boot needs to keep moisture from getting to the foot, but it also needs to breathe so the foot doesn't get swampy, as this can lead to discomfort and blisters. Waterproof boots won't breathe. For winter hikes and trails in wetlands, waterproof boots are a must, however.

- **Traction** – You want thick, nonskid rubber soles, which are good for keeping your footing on a variety of terrain, such as slippery wet rocks, mud and sand. The outsole, or the bottom front of the shoe that hits the terrain, should have deep indentations or grooves to improve your grip on slippery surfaces.

- **Durable** – The boot should last until the child outgrows them, or for about a year.

Both you and your kids always should wear your boots around the house and yard to break them in and so you can see if they fit properly before heading into the wilds. Afterward, check your feet and your kids' to see if there is any rubbing against the skin. Particularly look for redness on the top of the foot, the back of the heel near the Achilles tendon, and on the toes. Redness in any of those spots is a sign that the boot doesn't fit right. If that's the case, return the footwear and try another size or brand.

Half the battle with kids is getting them to like the boot you buy for them. You'll want to bring them along not just to try on the boot to see if it's a good fit but to purchase something they'll like.

Don't allow children to wear open-toed shoes on a hike. Sandals are fine for the beach and walks on paved surfaces but not for the woods where rocks, roots and bugs all can get at exposed toes.

Infants and toddlers confined to the baby carrier don't need hiking boots. Besides being heavy, their rigidness actually can harm developing feet. Sneakers are sufficient for the few minutes they come out of the carrier and get to run about the trail.

As kids' feet grow, you could find yourself buying new hiking boots a lot, probably a pair every year. You'll have to decide based on the trails you traverse and the frequency of your hikes if sneakers are good enough. To help keep costs down, you can waterproof kids' shoes with sprays, as a less expensive alternative to buying waterproof footwear.

Socks

Socks serve two purposes: to wick sweat away from skin and to provide cushioning. Cotton socks aren't very good for hiking, except in extremely dry environments, because they retain moisture that can result in blisters. Wool socks or liner socks work best. You'll want to look for three-season socks, also known as trekking socks. While a little thicker than summer socks, their extra cushioning generally prevents blisters.

Also, make sure kids don't put on holey socks; that's just inviting blisters.

Shorts or jeans?

So long as you don't go off trail, shorts are fine if the weather is warm enough. You'll want to make sure the kids use sunscreen and insect repellant on their legs, though.

Denim jeans are great during dry weather but become uncomfortable when wet. Because of this, some hikers prefer to wear nylon pants. I prefer not to take kids hiking when rain is falling, but trails in some areas of the nation – the Pacific Northwest for example – will be wet regardless if there's a shower.

During winter, wear long johns, preferably of a moisture-wicking synthetic material. Wool pants or trousers that are water resistant would go over them.

Shirts and jackets

Dress for the weather. For example, a light-colored and loose-fitting T-shirt is a must on hot, sunny summer days and in desert areas, a windbreaker a must in windy climes, and a water-resistant rain jacket in wet areas.

Some parents prefer to dress their kids in bright clothes on hikes, as they're easier to spot should they become lost or get injured and can't respond to your calls. Not all parents feel that way, though:

> *"As I hike with just my daughter and she's never out of my sight, I prefer to dress her in earth-tones – greens, beiges, tan, browns. Looking at a kid wearing pink or hunter orange in the wilds is an intrusion upon my enjoyment of nature." –*
> *Julio S., Austin, Texas*

Layering

On all but the hot, dry days, you and your children should wear multiple layers of clothing that provide various levels

CLOTHING

of protection against sweat, heat loss, wind and potentially rain. Layering works because the type of clothing you select for each stratum serves a different function, such as wicking moisture or shielding against wind. In addition, trapped air between each layer of clothing is warmed by the child's body heat. Layers also can be added or taken off as needed.

Generally, both you and a child need three layers. Closest to your skin is the wicking layer, which pulls perspiration away from the body and into the next layer, where it evaporates. Exertion from walking means you will sweat and generate heat, even if the weather is cold. The second layer is an insulation layer, which helps keep you warm. The last layer is a water-resistant shell that protects you from rain, wind, snow and sleet.

As the seasons and weather change, so does the type of clothing you select for each layer. The first layer ought to be a loose-fitting T-shirt in summer, but in winter and on other cold days you might opt for a long-sleeved moisture-wicking synthetic material, like polypropylene. During winter, the next layer probably also should cover the neck, which often is exposed to the elements. A turtleneck works fine, but preferably not one made of cotton, as this won't wick moisture from the skin when you sweat. The third layer in winter, depending on the temperature, could be a wool sweater, a half-zippered long sleeved fleece jacket, or a fleece vest.

You might even add a fourth layer of a hooded parka with pockets, made of material that can block wind and resist water. Gloves or mittens as well as a hat also are necessary on cold days.

Headgear

Half of all body heat is lost through the head, hence the hiker's adage, "If your hands are cold, wear a hat." In cool, wet weather, wearing a hat is at least good for avoiding hypothermia, a potentially deadly condition in which heat loss occurs faster than the body can generate it. Children are more susceptible to hypothermia than adults.

In lower latitudes, higher altitudes, deserts and especially during summer, a hat with a wide brim is useful in keeping the sun out of your eyes. It's also nice should rain start to fall.

Wear lightweight hats in late spring and summer and heavier ones in cooler weather. During winter, wear balaclavas or hats with ear flips.

For young children, get a hat with a chin strap. They like to play with their hats, which will fly off in a wind gust if not "fastened" some way to the child.

Sunglasses

Sunglasses are an absolute must at high altitudes, if walking through open areas exposed to the sun, and in winter when children can suffer from snow blindness. Look for 100% UV-protective shades, which provide the best screen.

The variety of sunglasses available out there are enormous, but when children are involved, always opt for something sturdy. You can buy sunglasses with no hinges, which means toddlers have one less avenue for breaking them. You even can buy symmetrical sunglasses that can

A hat with a wide brim provides excellent protection against the sun, even on little tykes.

be worn either right-side-up or upside down (for some reason, toddlers like to wear sunglasses upside down). These options also cost more money than an inexpensive pair you can buy for kids at any discount store. Also, be prepared for children to lose their sunglasses.

Rain gear

A water-resistant poncho is sufficient most of the time for children on a day hike. But if the temperature falls into the 50s or lower, or if hiking in a place that sees a lot of rainfall or that is windy, more elaborate gear – such as a rain jacket and rain pants – will be better. Other rain gear might include water-resistant boots and a rain hat with a wide brim. As I advise against hiking on rainy days, we won't spend much time on this topic. Still, carry a poncho or hooded, water-resistant windbreaker with you for each child on overcast days.

Winter wear

For the northern United States, winter as well as early spring and late autumn require cold-weather clothing. Besides layering with thicker clothing or even adding a fourth layer, you'll want to wear gloves or mittens. The latter is better for children as they keep the fingers grouped together and so warmer. Scarves or mufflers are needed to the cover neck. Always bring extra shirts, socks and even shoes to change into after the hike. Shoes likely will get wet on a cold weather hike, and children will need new socks so they don't have to suffer through cold feet on the drive home.

After the hike

Even if the weather is warm, bring a complete change of clothes, including footwear, for each child, just in case.

CLOTHING

The clothes don't have to be those that the kids would wear in the wilds. If all goes well on the hike, you won't need to change clothes, but it's best to be prepared.

Chapter 5: Equipment

Hiking isn't like taking a walk at the city park. You'll potentially encounter rough terrain, and because you're in a remote area with limited or even no public amenities, you will need to bring supplies, even if you'll be gone just for the afternoon. This is especially true when children are with you. Among the equipment you'll need are those items that allow you to carry these various supplies, such a backpack and canteens, and a way to help you traverse the wilds, such as a trekking pole.

Always try on and practice using your gear before hitting the trail. Besides saving you a lot of time adjusting straps and trying to figure out how something works while anxious kids want to start walking, the practice will give you an opportunity to see if you really have the right equipment. If you don't, return it immediately, replace it with something else, and practice again.

What you'll need

A couple of principles will guide your purchases. First, the longer and more complex the hike, the more equipment you'll need. Secondly, your general goal is to go light. Since you're on a day hike, the amount of gear you'll need is a fraction of what backpackers shown in magazines and catalogs usually carry. Indeed, the inclination of most day hikers is to not carry enough equipment. For the lightness

EQUIPMENT

issue, most gear today is made with titanium and siliconized nylon, ensuring it is study and fairly light. While the list of what you need may look long, it won't weigh much.

Baby carriers

If your child is an infant or toddler, you'll have to carry him. Until infants can hold their heads up, which usually doesn't happen until about four to six months of age, a front pack (like a Snugli or Baby Bjorn) is best. It keeps the infant close for warmth and balances out your backpack. At same time, though, you must watch for baby overheating in a front pack, so you'll need to remove the infant from your body at rest stops.

When purchasing a front pack, you'll want one with padded straps if walking for any long distance, or they'll start digging into your shoulders. Make sure the front pack provides good neck and head support for baby. Also, look for one that isn't too difficult to put on. Some have a number of straps on them that you'll constantly have to adjust as baby grows.

Once children reach about 20 pounds, they typically can hold their heads up and sit on their own. At that point, you'll want a baby carrier (sometimes called a child carrier or baby backpack), which can transfer the infant's weight to your hips when you walk. You'll not only be comfortable, but your child will love it, too.

Look for a baby carrier that is sturdy yet lightweight. Your child is going to get heavier as time passes, so about the only way you can counteract this is to reduce the weight of the items you use to carry things. The carrier also should have adjustment points, as you don't want your child to outgrow the carrier too soon. A padded waist belt and padded shoulder straps are necessary for your comfort. The carrier should provide some kind of head and neck support if you're hauling an infant. It also should offer back support for children of all ages, and leg holes should be wide enough so there's no chafing. You also want to be able to load your infant without help. It also should be stable enough to stand so when you take it off the child can sit in it for a moment while you get turned around. You don't want a carrier that you must swing around your back to put on. Instead, you should be able to sit down, pull the carrier onto your back as you adjust the straps, and then stand.

Stay away from baby carriers with only shoulder straps as you need the waist belt to help shift the child's weight to your hips for more comfortable walking. Older "Gerry" baby carriers from yard sales also are a no-no. They were recalled because when small infants shifted to one side they could slip through the leg openings to the ground.

Many carriers come with extras. I generally eschew the add-ons as they unnecessarily increase the carrier's weight. The most any person can carry on their back about 60 pounds, and beginning hikers probably won't be able to haul much more than 30-35 pounds, which is about the weight of a toddler and their carrier.

Still, sun and rain guards as well as canopies are popular, even though they generally don't provide the perfect sun and wind protection as claimed, for at just the right angle (which almost always seems to be the angle the trail takes), the elements still can get in. Children usually

EQUIPMENT

A baby carrier provides a perfect way to bring infants and toddlers on long hikes. The carrier is worn like a backpack.

don't like looking through plastic windows, which often become scratched and discolored after a few hikes. In addition, they can be awkward to assemble and can't be easily stowed on the trail if you want to take them on and off. A simple hat with a wide brim and properly layered clothing will keep sun and wind off your child while giving an unhindered view. In some regions, like the

Pacific Northwest, hiking without risk of rain may be impossible for long stretches of time, so you'll have to decide if the benefits of this add-on outweigh the negatives.

Another add-on are stirrups. Feet can dangle, and though kids may prefer that, stirrups are helpful once they start kicking about. Kids in baby carriers do swing their legs, and their feet can hit you hard in the back or ribs.

Places to strap things on and extra pockets are fun, but I prefer a fanny pack. To reach anything on a baby carrier, you'll have to take it off, and that is inconvenient when hiking with children.

Hiking with a baby carrier poses different challenges than backpacks, mainly because your child will move about as you walk, which can throw you off balance, especially on steep or rocky terrain. Seated children will have a lower center of gravity than a full backpack, and this makes achieving a good weight distribution difficult if sometimes not impossible. In addition, you can't scoot down rocks or inclines on your butt as your child's feet are under you and would be crushed.

You'll need to learn how to walk with a baby carrier, so before hitting the trail it's a good idea to place your child in one, put it on, and try vacuuming (to simulate the bending you'll need to do on ascents) and walking around your neighborhood. It's a good conversation starter with the neighbors and certain to earn you and your child friendly waves.

Seat the infant or toddler in the carrier each time before heading on a hike so you can readjust the straps for both the child and for you. This only takes a few minutes to do and will save you much trouble during the hike.

EQUIPMENT

If the day is a bit cool, a child in a carrier will need to be dressed slightly warmer than you are. Children in carriers will get cold because they're not exerting themselves as you are on the trail. They also could be more exposed to the wind depending on your direction of travel. On the other hand, if the day is a bit on the warm side, children on your back may need to be dressed cooler than you as the nylon making up a carrier seat doesn't breathe. Some hikers recommend jury-rigging umbrellas on the carrier to keep the child out of the sun, but if a sunhat isn't enough to protect your child, then you probably are hiking in too hot of weather for a kid. If walking in an area where you'll be exposed to direct sunlight, make sure they wear a hat and that their hands, legs and feet are covered in clothing or sunscreen.

Before setting out on the trail, always be sure to buckle up your child by using the carrier's shoulder straps. Their squirming about increases their chance of falling out if they aren't strapped in.

Be aware that during the hike younger children like to take off their sunhat and sunglasses just out of curiosity or because they're uncomfortable in them. They end up dropping them on the trail and then run the risk of sunburn or of being blinded by sunlight. You'll need to periodically look back over your shoulder and see that they still have their head and eye protection on. Their legs also may be exposed as baby and toddler pants creep up.

The child also will need to be taken out of the carrier for every hour you walk. This will give you a rest stop and give the toddler a chance to run around, which he'll welcome.

You'll need to stop using the baby carrier when one of two milestones are reached: Your children outgrow it (in either weight or height), which for average-size kids happens sometime during their third year, or when your children become too heavy for you to comfortably carry them. You'll then need to start having your child walk. That most likely will mean cutting back on the distance you can traverse. When my son was two, we'd peakbag mountains on six-mile hikes with him in the carrier the whole way, but by the time he was four, we were limited to two-mile, fairly flat trails. The good news is as children age they can go a little farther every year.

Just because the child can walk doesn't mean you should quit wearing a baby carrier, though:

"By about the middle of my son's third year, he could scramble over any terrain and weighed 40 pounds, so I had him walk; fortunately, he wanted to be on the ground so he could explore the fascinating world around him; I still took the carrier along with me, just in case he tired out or was injured in some way, necessitating that I carry him out." – Sara F., Lebanon, N.H.

If a baby carrier sounds like a lot of work, consider this: a full pack to go in the backcountry usually weighs about 45 pounds. Your child won't weigh 45 until he's in his fours. An infant weighing under 20 pounds is nothing to carry on one's back, even if you add the four or five pounds of the carrier to it. In addition, most infants and toddlers like to be in baby carriers. They can see the world from a higher vantage point and can make direct eye contact with others.

EQUIPMENT

Some casual day hikers will want to use strollers rather than baby carriers. This is fine in paved urban areas but will be nearly impossible on wild trails. The surface will be too rough, eating up the strollers' plastic wheels. Other surfaces will be sandy or rocky, making pushing a stroller difficult at best.

Fanny packs

Also known as a belt bag, a fanny pack is virtually a must for anyone with a baby carrier as you can't otherwise lug a backpack. If your significant other is with you, he or she can carry the backpack, of course. Still, the fanny pack also is a good alternative to a backpack in hot weather, as it will reduce back sweat.

If you have only one or two kids on a hike, or if they also are old enough to carry daypacks, your fanny pack need not be large. A mid-size pouch can carry at least 200 cubic inches of supplies, which despite this book's seemingly extensive list of sundries you should carry, is more than enough to accommodate them all:

> *"The fanny pack is the easiest way to carry anything on the trail. Mine has one zipper that opens to a single pouch, in which I've lined up everything needed, from first-aid kit to trail mix. I have one with canteens on both sides of the pouch, which makes getting water convenient."*
> *– Mary W., Asheville, N.C.*

Some fanny packs even come with a CD/MP3 player pocket and headphone port, but there's really no need for such add-ons. You want to be able to hear your children at least for safety purposes, and you might even want to talk with them. In any case, if one of the points of the hike is to commune with nature, how can you do that if the latest music of our highly technical world is pounding in your ears?

Backpacks

Sometimes called daypacks for day hikes or for kids, backpacks are essential once kids come down from the baby carrier. As the child is older and requires more, you'll need to find a better way to carry all of the essentials you need – snacks, first-aid kit, extra clothing – than a fanny pack.

With multiple children, fanny packs can get awful crowded, so every time you dig through them, whatever you've packed gets knocked out of place. That makes finding an item difficult the next time you need it and increases the chances of losing something. Fanny packs also can carry only so much, so upsizing has it limits. By instead enlisting your back and shoulders, you can carry more items, a necessity the more children you have and the farther your hike goes.

Adult packs

For day hike purposes with children, you'll want to get yourself an internal frame, in which the frame giving the backpack its shape is inside the pack's fabric so it's not exposed to nature. Such frames usually are lightweight and comfortable. External frames have the frame outside the pack, so they are exposed to the elements. They are excellent for long hikes into the backcountry when you must carry heavy loads.

EQUIPMENT

When purchasing a backpack, you'll first need to find the right size. Measure your back from the vertebrae at the neck's base to the point in the small of your back that is level with the top of the hipbones and then examine the backpack tags to see which one matches your length. Next, look for padded straps and a padded waist belt for comfort and sewed joints to ensure sturdiness.

Always fit yourself for a backpack before buying it. Select one that rides comfortably on your back, that doesn't chafe, and that doesn't stress the shoulders and pull on your neck. When fitting it, load it lightly. Stores usually have pillows and sacks for doing this. Adjust the straps. The shoulder straps should be snug but allow your arms to move freely while the hip belt should rest comfortably on your hipbones.

Ensure that your backpack will have enough space to carry the essentials (more on this later) and that there is extra space to haul those items that younger kids decide they're not going to carry anymore. Lighter packs mean less stress on knees, back, shoulders and neck. They also mean you can walk more quickly to safety.

A couple of final thoughts: If buying a backpack secondhand for either you or a child, make sure the material isn't wearing thin and that the straps and joints are still in good shape. Also, if a backpack has metal zippers, consider replacing the pulls with cloth ribbons. The metal can get cold in wet weather and low temps.

<u>Kid's packs</u>

As kids get older, and especially after they've been hiking for a couple of years, they'll soon want a "real" backpack. It's a good idea to get kids carrying a small daypack with a couple of light items in it by the time they're in elementary school. If you don't get them to realize they have a responsibility to carry their own stuff, they'll balk at doing so later. Fortunately, most young children want to wear their own daypack so they can be like the adult. That's good. It will help keep them physically fit and teaches them self-reliance and planning.

Unfortunately, most backpacks for kids are overbuilt and too heavy. Even light ones that safely can hold up to 50 pounds are inane for most children.

When buying a daypack for your child, look for sternum straps, which help keep the strap on the shoulders. This is vital for prepubescent children as they do not have the broad shoulders that come with adolescence, meaning packs likely will slip off and onto their arms, making them uncomfortable and difficult to carry. Don't buy a backpack that a child will "grow into." Backpacks that don't fit well simply will lead to sore shoulder and back muscles and could result in poor posture.

Also, consider purchasing a daypack with a hydration system for kids. This will help ensure they drink a lot of water. More on this later when we get to canteens.

Inexpensive school backpacks available at discount department stores usually are sufficient for hiking. All are lightweight, coming in at roughly 18 ounces, and all have a small amount of space so children can't carry too much. The cost can be at least half of a sports store backpack. Of course, they also may look comparatively silly in the woods – do you really want your daughter hiking with a Barbie backpack?

EQUIPMENT

When should your children carry their own stuff and how much should they carry? Infants through 4 year olds shouldn't be expected to carry anything. Preschoolers might use a trekking pole or collect interesting stuff found on the way, but they probably won't carry any of it for long. Small frame packs are fine for healthy 5-7 year olds. A capacity internal frame pack is okay for 9-12 year olds.

Before hitting the trail, always check your children's backpacks to make sure that they have not overloaded them. Kids think they need more than they really do. They also tend to overestimate their own ability to carry stuff. Sibling rivalries often lead to children to packing more than they should in their rucksacks, too. Don't let them overpack "to teach them a lesson," though, as it can damage bones and turn the hike into a bad experience.

A good rule of thumb is no more than 25 percent capacity. Most upper elementary school kids can carry only about 10 pounds for any short distance. Subtract the weight of the backpack, and that means only 4-5 pounds in the backpack. Overweight children will need to carry a little less than this or they'll quickly be out of breath.

I've seen some formulas that say a child should be able to carry a pound of weight for every five pounds they weigh. A 90-pound child then would be able to carry 18 pounds. This formula seems overly optimistic, however. A physically fit, athletic teenager probably can carry this much, and as they near adulthood, more. But don't expect this of your fourth grader – and especially not of your preschooler.

Increase the amount that children carry as they grow and are capable of taking on more weight. Once a teenager, they can move up to small adult backpacks and carry some of the load that you usually take. Still, limit the amount your teens carried based on their abilities.

Alternatives

If you have a lot of children to watch or an injury that prevents you or a child from carrying a backpack, that doesn't mean the hike is over. Instead consider enlisting a "Sherpa," a friend who accompanies you to carry items. You do run the risk of talking with your Sherpa rather than bonding with your kids the length of the hike, though. Perhaps if you have teenagers among your children, one of them can act as Sherpa. Another option is to bring a dog that can carry items, though this is not always practical, as it may not be suited for such work. A lot of places you might hike won't allow dogs. In addition, if you bring a dog, you've got to plan for its food, water and potty needs as well, which only adds to what must be carried.

Canteens

Canteens or plastic bottles filled with water are vital for any hike, no matter how short the trail. You'll need to have enough of them to carry about 2 pints of water per person for every hour of hiking. If going into arid regions, you'll probably need more.

When looking for a canteen or a water bottle, make sure it seals tight and can be stored upright in a carrying case. The carrying case should hook to your backpack or fanny pack belt. You don't want to place canteens or water bottles loose in your backpack, or they could drip, leaving your gear and extra clothing wet.

EQUIPMENT

Another possibility – and one popular with kids – is a hydration system. A lightweight plastic bag connected to a plastic tube can be filled with water and placed inside a daypack or a fanny pack (some backpacks come with them built in). The child then can drink water as walking simply by sucking on a tube, as if an astronaut in a space capsule. Since it's so effortless to use, kids tend to stay hydrated with it. Some hydration systems will hold up to 35 ounces of water, which is little more than a quart.

Trekking poles

Also known as walking sticks, hiking sticks or walking poles, trekking poles are necessary for maintaining stability on uneven or wet surfaces and to help reduce fatigue. The latter makes them useful on even surfaces. By transferring weight to the arms, a trekking pole can reduce stress on knees and lower back, allowing you to maintain a better posture and to go farther.

Trekking poles have some other benefits beyond keeping your balance. If forced to stay the night in the wilds, a stick can be used to build a makeshift tent. It also can be used to fight off attacking animals.

As an adult with a baby or toddler on your back, you'll primarily want a trekking pole to help you maintain your balance, even if on a flat surface, and to help absorb some of the impact of your step.

Graphite tips provide the best traction. A basket just above the tip is a good idea so the stick doesn't sink into mud or sand. Angled cork handles are ergonomic and help absorb sweat from your hands so they don't blister. A strap on the handle to wrap around your hand is useful so the stick doesn't slip out. Telescopic poles are a good idea as you can adjust them as needed based on the terrain you're hiking and as kids grow to accommodate their height. The pole also needs to be sturdy enough to handle rugged terrain, as you don't want a pole that bends when you press it to the ground. Spring-loaded shock absorbers help when heading down a steep incline but aren't necessary. Indeed, for a short walk across flat terrain, the right length stick is about all you need.

When hiking, take off any tip protectors that come with the pole. Usually these protectors are included so the sharp tip doesn't cut or scratch other objects while you're traveling. You probably don't need such a sharp tip on a pole when hiking with kids, but should you have one, definitely make sure kids don't horse around with the pole.

You may have seen pictures of hikers using two trekking poles, as if they were skiing. Having two poles works well on long backcountry treks and over steep terrain, but you probably will only need one pole on your day hike. I myself like to have one hand free in case I need to hold my child's hand or help him up or down an embankment.

Children don't really need trekking poles unless tackling steep or uneven terrain, but they'll likely want one to look like an adult. Kids as young as three can use trekking poles. You will need to adjust it to their height, though.

If buying a trekking pole for a child, make sure the grip isn't too large for them, as children have smaller hands than adults. Next check the length. Holding the child's arm out at a right angle (with the elbow the bend) in front of them, adjust the pole length so that the tip reaches the child's ankle.

You'll have to show most children how to use the trekking pole, or they'll soon be dragging them behind them. Prepare for younger kids to misuse trekking poles, which they find are great for whacking plants, trees, rocks and even siblings.

Also be prepared to eventually carry a young child's trekking pole, even if they're still on the ground. They'll grow tired of carrying it (or playing with it). Velcro leather pieces that bicyclists use for their wrists are perfect for securing their trekking pole to a carrier or backpack.

Multi-purpose tool

Though rarely used on day hikes, a multi-purpose tool (a Swiss Army knife is a type of one) is indispensable. It has a number of gizmos on it, such as scissors, awl, corkscrew, bottle cap opener and wire cutters, any of which could prove useful should you end up spending the night in the wilds. When buying a multi-purpose tool, look for a one that as a minimum has a small knife, scissors and screwdriver. You probably don't need much more. Try to find one that is small and lightweight.

A number of parent hikers say a knife also is a must, and it is indeed a handy tool in case of an emergency. With a multi-purpose tool, however, you won't really need a knife. Other parents like to carry a knife for whittling. That's not a great idea, though, as a knife can slip, leaving a gash in a palm or finger. In the past, use of a knife may have been one of those unofficial rites of passages into manhood, but today different attitudes prevail:

> *"I carry a very small pocketknife on my multi-purpose tool and never make a show of it in front of my son, who is only a preschooler. Kids shouldn't play with them lest they injure themselves." – Scott O., Portland, Maine*

If you do carry a large knife, making sure it has a locking blade.

Carabiners

Carabiners are metal loops, vaguely shaped like a D, with a sprung or screwed gate. You'll find that hooking a couple of them to your back or fanny pack useful in many ways. For example, if you need to dig through a fanny pack, you can hook the strap of your trekking pole to it. Your hat, camera straps, first-aid kit and a number of other objects also can connect to them. Hook them to your fanny pack or backpack upon purchasing them, so you don't forget them when packing. Small carabiners with sprung gates are inexpensive, but they do have a limited life span of a couple of dozen hikes.

Waterproof bags

You'll want to have on hand waterproof bags for holding packed extra clothing and a variety of other items. If rain should fall or your backpack tumbles into a stream or lake, those clothes will be protected so you can remain dry.

Rope

This is one of those items you'll probably never need, but should you be forced to stay the night, it will make building a shelter much easier. As with a multi-purpose tool's many gadgets, you never know when one will come in handy. You don't need anything too expensive. Ten to 12 feet of nylon cord will be more than sufficient. To help cut costs, clothesline rope also will work.

Camera

Take plenty of pictures. You later can look at them with your children and talk about what you saw. They can be used to make a scrapbook or posted on social networks like Facebook. Teenagers might even want to create a blog about their hikes.

Go for durability and lightness in a camera. That probably means taking a digital camera, which has the advantage of no film or extra lenses to carry. It doesn't have to be a simple point-and-shoot. Find one that also can take videos, and you're set.

Make sure you get a waterproof camera case that can strap to your belt, and wear it on the side of your hip. Don't forget spare batteries.

Having said all of this, if photography is a hobby of yours and you don't mind lugging around equipment that can come with a single lens reflex camera, a hike certainly is a great place to find fantastic vistas and scenery for pictures. Bring along the equipment with young kids, however, and you might truly find your hands full.

Camping gear

For many, hiking is an extension of camping – that is, it's something to do between nights of sleeping in a tent.

Make Your Own Gear

You can help kids craft their own equipment for the hike using materials found in your own home.

Trekking pole
■ **Materials** – Stick, knife for carving wood, sandpaper, wood finish
■ **Instructions** – (1) Walk with your children into your yard, if you have a lot of trees, or to a nearby woods. Each child than can pick a stick that their hand can fit nicely around and that comes up to their hips. (2) At home, carve off bark and sand it. (3) Stain it with a brown or reddish-brown finish. They now have a hiking stick. Most children can't wait to use it.

Utility belt pockets
■ **Materials** – Craft knife, duct tape, scissors
■ **Instructions** – (1) Lay out a foot-long strip of duct tape, sticky side up. (2) About halfway down this strip, place a second strip sticky side down. (3) Turn over the strips then halfway down the second strip stick a third piece. (4) Repeat steps 1-3 until you have a sheet about three quarters the height of the item to be carried. (5) Fold over the top and bottom sticky edges of this duct tape sheet then wrap it around the item to be carried. (6) If necessary, trim the sheet, then tape it in place to form a loose pocket. (7) Close the pocket's bottom with another piece of duct tape and trim the edges. (8) Slip a piece of scrap cardboard into each pocket as a temporary backing (for a stiffer backing, thin scrap wood also can be used). (9) Near the top of the pocket, with a craft knife cut two vertical slits about 1-1/2 inches apart and slightly longer than your child's belt is wide (if a child is making the

pocket, a parent should do this step). (10) Slide the pockets onto your child's belt.

Water bottle holder
- **Materials** – Duct tape, scissors, water bottle
- **Instructions** – Follow steps 1-4 for the utility belt pockets. (5) Fold up the bottom tape's edge and trim the two side edges so they're even. (6) Along the exposed top piece of tape, cut inch-wide tabs in the shape of an H. (7) Wrap the sheet around your child's water bottle with the tabs at the bottom, sticky sides out. (8) Trim the sheet then tape it in place to form a loose pocket around the bottle. (9) To create a bottom for the pocket, fold over the tabs, sticking each one to the next, then cover the tabs with more duct tape.

Camping involves a whole range of gear, such as tents, sleeping bags, sleeping mats, stoves, utensils, lanterns and more. It'll require much heavier loads to carry, or you might simply drive a vehicle full of the gear up to your campsite. You'll also probably have to pay for a campsite permit. As the scope of this book is limited to day hiking, in which you leave home after the sun has come up and return home before the sun goes down, we'll leave camping at that. You can consult guidebooks about camping to find out about what camping gear is best for children and other particulars of the pastime.

Winter gear

Crampons, ice axes, gaiters and snowshoes all are useful – but if a trail requires such equipment to traverse, wait until the children become teenagers before trying it. Such terrain is simply too difficult (and too unsafe) for younger children to cross.

Where to buy gear

A number of places exist where you can find this equipment, as well as clothing and other outdoor gear: sporting goods stores, discount stores, garage sales, family and friends, second-hand stores, Internet sale boards, and clubs. To cut your expenses, buy it on sale or off-season, which typically is January. If buying second-hand items, make sure they're still usable and comfortable.

Despite having served in the Army infantry, I'm not a big fan of military surplus gear. Most parents will find it bulky and cumbersome. Such gear really is suited for the rigors of the battlefield, not a family day hike. Having said this, I know a number of parent hikers who wouldn't go into the wilds without their Ranger pack.

You also might consider making your own gear. It's not necessarily less expensive than what you'll find on a store shelf, but constructing the equipment can be fun and teach your children some skills as well. A number of websites provide instructions on making everything from backpacks to hammocks. You'll need to have a sewing machine for a number of the projects.

Chapter 6: Navigational Tools

Without navigational tools such as a paper map or GPS, you can easily become disoriented, miss a turn and get lost. Many trails – even short loops – have branching and adjoining trails.

A map that gives you a sense of what is around you can help you better pinpoint your location. Sometimes you have to unexpectedly go off the main trail – it could be a trail closure, animal encounter, sudden change in the weather for the worse, or an injury that requires shortening the trip. A map also can help you better appreciate where you are by pointing out the names of geographic features you pass or see on the horizon.

Paper maps

Paper maps may sound passé in this age of GPS, but you'll find the variety and breadth of view they offer to be useful. During the planning process, a paper map (even if viewing it online), will be far superior to a GPS device. On the hike, you'll also want a backup to GPS. Or like many casual hikers, you may not own GPS at all, which makes paper maps indispensable.

Types of maps

Different types of maps each offer advantages and disadvantages when planning your hike and out on the trail.

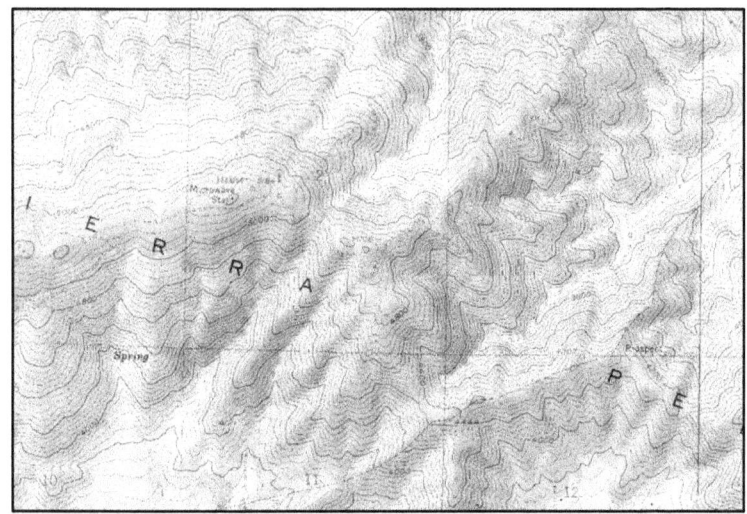

A topographical map provides details about the landscape that are invaluable to a hiker.

Standard road map (also printed guides and handmade trail maps)

These maps show highways and locations of cities and parks. Maps included in guidebooks, printed guides handed out at parks, and that are hand drawn tend to be designed like road maps, and often carry the same positives and negatives.

The main advantage of a standard road map is that it eliminates all of the extraneous info you'll find on other maps, focusing on a key landmark feature, specifically roads. Because of this, a road map is mainly useful for helping you figure out how to reach the trailhead, and in the case of printed guides, pointing out highlights you can see on the trail.

The benefits end there, though. Standard road maps rarely show trails or forest roads that you might traverse.

NAVIGATIONAL TOOLS

In addition, they don't give you a sense of the lay of the land, such as how high hills and mountains are. If hand drawn, as are many of those on printed guides, they are not always done to scale, making any estimate of how far you've got to go difficult if not impossible.

<u>Topo maps</u>

Topographical maps give contour lines and other important details for crossing a landscape. You'll find them invaluable on a hike into the wilds.

The contour lines' shape and their spacing on a topo map show the form and steepness of a hill or mountains, unlike the standard road map and most brochures and handmade trail maps. You'll also know if you're in a woods, which is marked in green, or in a clearing, which is marked in white. If you get lost, figuring out where you are and how to get to where you need to be will be much easier with such information.

For some day hikes, though, this is information overload. If there's only one clearly marked trail on a flat surface, a topo map isn't all that necessary. Another disadvantage is if going on a long hike, you will need a couple of sheets or a large topo map to show the area where you're going, and this can be a bit cumbersome, especially in a breeze.

In addition, some U.S. Geological Survey topo maps are out of date and may not give the most current forest road or trail numbers.

Private companies often offer more up-to-date topo maps of major hiking areas like national parks. Still, for remote areas such as national forests and BLM land,

USGS maps tend to be accurate more often than not as the landscape hasn't significantly changed in decades.

Satellite photos

Sometimes a view from above that is rendered exactly as it would look from an airplane is useful. Thanks to Google and other online services, you can get fairly detailed pictures of the landscape. Such pictures are an excellent resource when researching a hiking trail.

Unfortunately, those pictures don't label what a feature is or what it's called, as would a topo map. Unless there's a stream, determining if a feature is a canyon bottom or a ridgeline also can be difficult. Like topo maps, satellite photos (most of which were taken by old Russian spy satellites), can be out of date a few years. Google satellite photos aren't in real time.

What kind of map should you carry? The answer is the best of each type, which is what I do. I like road maps to show me how to get to the trailhead and printed guides to give me an overview of the trail's key points. I like a satellite pic to show me where to park and how to reach the trailhead, as they are not always easy to visually locate. I use topo maps to show me the trail and landmarks on the horizon I can see to help orient myself. With a yellow highlighter I mark the trail and direction of travel on my topo map.

Fortunately, you don't need to spend any money on maps or mapping software. Road maps, topo maps and satellite pictures are all available online for free. If you're going to make a number of hikes in a specific area, such as

NAVIGATIONAL TOOLS

a national forest or a national park, purchasing a large map of that entire region can be useful in selecting a trail to hike, though.

When carrying paper maps, you'll want to place them in a waterproof bag. You can buy see-through map cases that string around your neck, which I recommend for those walking in rainy climates. Since you're mainly going to walk on sunny days, however, a quart-size re-sealable plastic storage bag (like Ziploc) usually is fine.

During the hike, you'll want to check your topo map regularly to make sure you're still on the right trail. Doing so at rest stops or at any fork in the path is a good idea.

Have your children carry duplicate copies of paper maps in their backpacks. Should yours get lost or wet, they'll then have one. If you have older teens, they even may need to use them in case you are injured. Paper also makes great tinder if you end up spending the night in the wilds and must make a fire; burning a duplicate map won't be a major loss to the expedition.

GPS

By using satellites, the global positioning system can find your spot on the Earth to within 10 feet. With a GPS device, you can preprogram the trailhead location and mark key turns and landmarks as well as the hike's end point. This mobile map is a powerful technological tool that almost certainly ensures you won't get lost – so long as you've correctly programmed the information. GPS also can calculate travel time and act as a compass, a barometer and altimeter, making such devices virtually obsolete on a hike.

In remote areas, however, reception is spotty at best for GPS, rendering your mobile map worthless. A GPS device also runs on batteries, and there's always a chance they will go dead. Or you may drop your device, breaking it in the process. Their screens are small, and sometimes you need a large paper map to get a good sense of the natural landmarks around you.

So which should you use, paper map or GPS? Simply put, GPS isn't enough. I recommend carrying both paper maps and GPS. Being a technogeek, I like to mainly use GPS, but there have been a number of times I was glad to have my paper topo map with me. Regardless, I do all of my planning on paper maps.

When buying a GPS device, the tradeoff almost always is between being lightweight and the number of functions it can perform. If you want to program in map routes and have a compass/altimeter/barometer, you'll need a heavier (or at least more expensive) model.

Familiarize yourself with the GPS device and practice using it, perhaps at a local playground, before heading into the wilds. The unit won't do you much good on the trail if you don't know how to use it. Finally, make sure you get a waterproof case for it.

Of course, to keep hiking inexpensive, you can dispense with GPS altogether. Paper maps and compass cost virtually nothing and do the same thing.

Compass

Like a paper map, a compass is indispensable even if you use GPS. Should your GPS no longer function, the compass then can be used to tell you which direction you're heading.

A protractor compass is best for hiking. Beneath the compass needle is a transparent base with lines to help your orient yourself. The compass often serves as a magnifying glass to help you make out map details. Most protractor compasses also come with a lanyard for easy carrying.

The compass and a map can be used in a number of ways, but the most basic skill (and you'll find the most useful on a day hike) is orienting the map properly. This will help you better understand which features are around you and give you a better idea of where the trail is heading. To do this, simply place your map on a flat surface. Next, place the compass on the map. Shift the map around until its line pointing "north" matches the north on your needle. The map is now oriented to the terrain.

A compass does have a one major issue: declination. Compass needles point at magnetic north, but maps use grid north. The difference in degrees between the two (usually listed on topo maps) is known as declination. You will have to rotate your compass dial to find grid north. If you don't, the discrepancy will cause you to walk several miles in the wrong direction. This usually is not significant on a day hike trail, but if the declination is large, you could become confused when taking a compass reading and comparing it to a map's grid north.

Another problem with compasses is field interference. Metal on your equipment can cause the needle to point the wrong direction. Always use a compass away from metal.

Guidebooks

Some hikers find information in them useful when out on the trail. While you might take kid-friendly field guides to help identify plants and animals, guidebooks about trails usually are bulky, and the first moment they get wet the pages turn moldy and curl out of shape. A guidebook is best left at home, if only to reduce the load you carry.

Bethany O., of Hood River, Ore., suggests:

> *"If there's information you need from a guidebook about a specific location, type it as notes and carry it with your paper maps. I usually do this for directions to the trailhead and location of key turns and landmarks to help me along the way."*

Chapter 7: Food and Water

Water is a necessity of any hiking trip, and food is a must if you're heading out with kids. To remain hydrated, adults and children alike need to drink regularly. To keep kids' energy levels up, they'll need to enjoy snacks.

Arranging hikes between meal times always is good planning. You don't want children on the trail when their bodies tell them they should be at the dinner table. Leave for the trail after a meal so that food can settle during the drive, and always head for home to ensure they'll eat their next meal on time. Maintaining the routines and schedules of home will help prevent a number of attitude problems on the trail.

Also, be sure to carry water and refrigerated food in insulated pouches or containers. This will keep them cool and from spoiling.

Water

As water is the heaviest item you'll probably carry, there is a temptation to not take as much as one should. Don't skimp on the amount of water you bring, though; after all, it's the one thing your body most needs. It's always better to end up with extra water than returning to your vehicle dehydrated.

How much water should you take? Adults need at least a quart for every two hours hiking. Children need to drink about a quart every two hours of walking and more if the weather is hot, dry or cold and if at a high altitude. To keep kids hydrated, have them drink at every rest stop.

Don't presume there will be water on the hiking trail. Most trails outside of urban areas lack such public amenities. In addition, don't drink water from local streams, lakes, rivers or ponds. There's no way to tell if local water is safe or not. As soon as you have drunk half of your water supply, you should turn around for the vehicle.

> *"To be safe, keep extra water in the car just in case you underestimate the amount of water needed or if canteen spills leave you short on water during the hike. Water could be frozen in bottles so that when you arrive back at your vehicle, it's still cold but melted." – Walt O., Bozeman, Mont.*

Bottled beverages containing juice or sports drinks are fine, but they also are no replacement for pure water. If your kids bring them, make sure they also drink water on the hike. In addition, don't let children bring boxed juice, which can easily spill and attract stinging insects.

Finally, remember that when children are young you'll need to carry their water as well. Accommodate for that in your packing.

Milk for infants

If you have an infant or unweaned toddler with you, milk is as necessary as water.

If bringing an infant or unweaned toddler, don't forget to carry milk or formula, a bottle and a nipple for milk breaks.

Children who only drink breastfed milk but don't have their mother on the hike requires that you have breast-pumped milk in an insulated beverage container (such as a Thermos) that can keep it cool to avoid spoiling. Know how much the child drinks and at what frequency so you can bring enough. You'll also need to carry the child's bottle and feeding nipples. Bring enough extra water in your canteen so you can wash out the bottle after each feeding. A handkerchief can be used to dry bottles between feedings.

If the child drinks powdered milk, you can premeasure the powder into a bottle or two then by shaking vigorously mix it with water as needed. Again, bring enough extra water for bottle washing.

Don't forget the baby's pacifier. Make sure it has a string and hook on it so it connects to the baby's outfit and isn't lost.

Food

> *"You were out far beyond civilization, and suddenly you heard five chocolate chip cookies calling you?"* – Charlie Brown (to Snoopy, who was out on a wilderness hike but then suddenly returned home)

Among the many wonderful things about hiking, at least for the kids, is that snacking between meals isn't frowned upon. Unless going on an all-day hike in which you'll picnic along the way, you want to keep them fed, as hungry children can lead to lethargy and whininess. It'll also keep young kids from snacking on the local flora or dirt. Before hitting the trail, you'll want to repackage as much of the food as possible as products sold at grocery stores tend to come in bulky packages that take up space and add a little weight to your backpack. Place the food in re-sealable plastic bags.

Snacks

Bring a variety of small snacks for rest stops. You don't want kids filling up on snacks, but you do need them to

FOOD AND WATER

maintain their energy levels if they're walking or to ensure they don't turn fussy if riding in a baby carrier. Go for complex carbohydrates and proteins for maintaining energy. Good options include dried fruits, jerky, nuts, peanut butter, prepared energy bars, candy bars with a high protein content (nuts, peanut butter), crackers, raisins and trail mix (called "gorp"). A number of trail mix recipes are available online; you and your children may want to try them out at home to see which ones you collectively like most.

Salty treats rehydrate better than sweet treats do. Chocolate and other sweets are fine if they're not all that's exclusively served, but remember they also tend to lead to thirst and to make sticky messes. Whichever snacks you choose, don't experiment with food on the trail. Bring what you know kids will like.

Give the first snack within a half-hour of leaving the trailhead or you risk children becoming tired and whiny from low energy levels. If kids start asking for them every few steps even after having something to eat at the last rest stop, consider timing snacks to reaching a seeable landmark, such as, "We'll get out the trail mix when we reach that bend up ahead."

How much food should you bring? Enough so each child can have a couple of snacks over a couple of miles is a good rule of thumb, but the older the child and the more difficult the terrain, the more food you'll likely need. Each child is different, of course, and may require more or less as the eating habits and metabolism dictate.

Many hikers use food to create a fond memory of hiking:

Trail Mix Recipes

Have kids help you make homemade trail mix, also known among backpackers as gorp.

Gorp
- **Ingredients** – 1 cup salted peanuts, 1 cup raisins, 1 cup M&Ms
- **Preparation** – Mix in a large bowl. Add other ingredients (sunflower seeds, cashews, granola) as you and your children desire. Portion out.

Kiddie Mix
- **Ingredients** – 4 cups of Chex cereal, 1/2 cup of dried fruit bits (apple chips, banana chips, or dried cranberries), 1/2 cup raisins, 1/2 cup salted peanuts, 1/2 cup M&Ms
- **Preparation** – Mix in a large bowl or pour into a gallon-size re-sealable zipper bag and shake.

Gorp Balls
- **Ingredients** – 1/3 cup each raisins, apple chips, dried apricots, dates and coconut, 1/2 cup sesame seeds, 1/3 cup walnuts, 2 cups peanuts, 1 cup chocolate chips, 1/3 cup honey, 1/2 cup peanut butter
- **Preparation** – In a large bowl, mix all ingredients, except for chocolate chips, honey and peanut butter. In another bowl, melt chocolate chips, honey and peanut butter for a minute in microwave. Mix the two bowls of ingredients. Shape mixture into balls. Refrigerate to harden.

"Bring a special snack to enjoy upon reaching your destination. When my two daughters and I hit the summit or take a break at the waterfall

FOOD AND WATER

we've just walked an hour or more to see, we break out a package of freeze-dried blueberry cheesecake. After a long hike, it's like eating in a gourmet restaurant." – Jackie S., Brevard, N.C.

Picnic lunch

If bringing a picnic lunch, you'll want to make sure the food is kept in insulated containers so it stays cool enough not to spoil. Also, keep food in solid, tightly sealed containers so they don't leak, get squashed, or attract animals when you take off your backpack at a rest stop. There's no need to give up your lunch to a clever squirrel.

When selecting a place to picnic, first consider the weather. If hot, get shade, and if breezy, find trees or boulders that serve as a wind break. Next, make sure there are no bugs nearby, particularly ants. This makes sandy ground and trees with sap bad places to picnic. Look for an area free of branches and sharp rocks, which will make sitting uncomfortable. Finally, pick a spot with a good, memorable view. You might be lucky enough to hike a trail with picnic tables, but the farther you go into the backcountry, the chances of finding one are nil.

There are a number of easy picnic lunches you can bring:

- **Tuna fish sandwich** – Carry a self-opening can of tuna and mayo packets like those found at fast food restaurants. Do some creative mixing in a plastic bag then place the tuna fish atop crackers or a whole wheat mini bagel. You can carry bread, too, but it is likely to get squished.

- **Other sandwiches** – Spread peanut butter, jams, jellies or cheese over hard crackers. Ship biscuits work quite well.
- **Salami sandwich** – Salami tends to last a long time, even in hot weather. It tastes great on hard rolls or crackers. Bologna usually doesn't last in warm weather.
- **Jerky with cheese and crackers** – Various jerky make a great, high protein meat to serve with crackers and cheese.

Add dried fruit and cookies or a candy bar for desert to any of these meals. Be aware that chocolate can melt in the heat, so it needs to be placed in an insulated container and kept cool.

Don't forget to bring napkins and a blanket or table cloth with you.

What not to bring

Avoid soda and other caffeinated beverages, alcohol, and energy pills. The caffeine will dehydrate children as well as you. Alcohol has no place on the trail; you need your full faculties when making decisions and driving home. Energy pills essentially are a stimulant and like alcohol can lead to bad calls. If you're tired, get some sleep and hit the trail another day.

Leftovers

Remember that you'll need to pack out wrappers, baggies and uneaten food. Burying them isn't a good idea as animals often will dig them up, leaving that section of the wood littered with trash.

Chapter 8: Sundries

The equipment you buy for hiking largely is meant for carrying around supplies you need to get by while in the wilds – the canteen holds water, the baby carrier holds your child, and the backpack holds ... well, whatever you need to survive with maybe a couple of "luxury" items like a journal or a good book.

When deciding what to bring, your mantra should be "Keep it light." The more you carry, the longer it will take you to get somewhere. The more weight on your back, the greater the chance of slipping and injuring yourself. Pack only essentials items, favoring those items with multiple uses. A multi-purpose tool, for example, can take the place of a scissors, a tweezers and a knife.

In this chapter, we'll explore what are the musts, the maybes and the never brings of your day hike.

Musts

You may never need any of these items while hiking, but the one time you do, you'll be glad they were available. My wife often jokes that because I carry them, I'll never need them.

First-aid kit
After water, this is the most essential item you can carry.

A few basic first-aid items can address a number of injuries, from bug and snake bites to cuts and broken bones.

A first-aid kit should include:
- Adhesive bandages of various types and sizes, especially butterfly bandages (for younger kids, make sure they're colorful kid bandages)
- Aloe vera
- Anesthetic (such as Benzocaine)
- Antacid (tablets)
- Antibacterial (aka antibiotic) ointment (such as Neosporin or Bacatracin)
- Anti-diarrheal tablets (for adults only, as giving this to a child is controversial)
- Anti-itch cream or calamine lotion
- Antiseptics (such as hydrogen peroxide, iodine or Betadine, Mercuroclear, rubbing alcohol)
- Baking soda
- Breakable (or instant) ice packs
- Cotton swabs

SUNDRIES

- Disposable syringe (w/o needle)
- Epipen (if children or adults have allergies)
- Fingernail clippers (your multi-purpose tool might have this, and if so you can dispense with it)
- Gauze bandage
- Gauze compress pads (2x2 individually wrapped pad)
- Hand sanitizer (use this in place of soap)
- Liquid antihistamine (not Benadryl tablets, however, as children should take liquid not pills; be aware that liquid antihistamines may cause drowsiness)
- Medical tape
- Moisturizer containing an anti-inflammatory
- Mole skin
- Pain reliever (a.k.a. aspirin; for children's pain relief, use liquid acetaminophen such Tylenol or liquid ibuprofen; never give aspirin to a child under 12)
- Poison ivy cream (for treatment)
- Poison ivy soap
- Powdered sports drinks mix or electrolyte additives
- Sling
- Snakebite kit
- Thermometer
- Tweezers (your multi-purpose tool may have this allowing you to dispense with it)
- Water purification tablets

If infants are with you, be sure to also carry teething ointment (such as Orajel) and diaper rash treatment.

Many of the items should be taken out of their store packaging to make placement in your fanny pack or backpack easier. In addition, small amounts of some items – such as baking soda and cotton swabs – can be placed inside re-sealable plastic bags, since you won't need the whole amount purchased.

Why you need each of these items may not be clear now, but when we reach Chapter 13 on Medical Problems, you'll see that each of them is in some way used during the treatment of an injury.

Make sure the first-aid items are in a waterproof container. A re-sealable plastic zipper bag is perfectly fine. If you hike in a humid climate like the Midwest or Southeast, be sure to replace the adhesive bandages every couple of months, as they can deteriorate in the moistness. Also, check your first-aid kit every few trips and after any hike in which you've just used it, so that you can replace used components and to make sure medicines haven't expired.

If you have older elementary-age kids and teenagers who've been trained in first aid, giving them a kit to carry as well as yourself is a good idea. Should they find themselves lost or you cannot get to them for a few moments, the kids might need to provide very basic first aid to one another.

Mobile phone

Carrying a mobile phone always is a good idea one in case you need to make an emergency phone call. If possible, you always should call a responsible party to let them know when you've arrived at your trailhead. Be aware that a mobile phone may not have reception in many remote areas. In addition, there probably is no way to recharge your phone other than through your vehicle, so take care of that before leaving home.

SUNDRIES

Also, remember that you're on a nature trail, not a city sidewalk:

> *"When on the trail, put away the mobile phone. The object of the adventure is to spend time with your kids and to enjoy nature. Use it only for emergencies. If you must take a phone call on the trail, be discrete as other hikers may hear your conversations."* – Mark P., Rapid City, S.D.

Wristwatch

A wristwatch may seem redundant in the age of mobile phones, but if your phone goes dead or is lost, a watch lets you know what time it is. This can be valuable in helping you gauge how far you've traveled. For example, if you know your brood covers about half a mile every half hour, and only 15 minutes have passed, then you've probably traveled a quarter mile. If you're lost, you'll need to know how soon you should think about going into emergency mode and staying the night in the wilds.

Wear a watch with hands, not a digital one. While digital watches come with all kinds of gizmos, like a barometer, altimeter and compass, most of them require a battery, and batteries have a way of going dead just when you need them most.

In case your GPS dies or you lose your compass, a wristwatch with hands also can be used to tell direction. Simply point the watch's hour hand toward the sun. Now imagine a line between the hour hand and the 12 on your watch; that line is true south. If you're currently on daylight savings time (in the United States, this is from the second Sunday of March to the day before the first Sunday of November, except Hawaii and the non-Navajo sections of Arizona), you'll need to pretend the hour hand is one hour earlier than it appears on your watch (so if the hour hand is on 11, pretend it's on 10). If cloudy, simply line up the hour hand with the brightest part of the sky.

Finally, make sure your watch is waterproof or water resistant. You don't want it to stop working during the rain or in case you accidentally take it into the water.

Prescriptions

Always bring on a hike any medicine regularly taken by children. Make sure they take the proper amounts when scheduled. You may need to bring a spoon or small medicine cup, if the medication is a liquid. Even if the medication isn't to be taken during the hike, should you be forced to stay a night in the wilds your children then will not go without.

Sunscreen, lip balm

Except in the Pacific Northwest, trails rarely are covered entirely in shade, so your child will need protection from the sun for both skin and lips.

For sunscreen, use a low scent/no scent variety. Scents can attract insects (leading to other issues) and even bears (really leading to other issues). Use a children's sunscreen rather than one for adults, as some kids' skin can be sensitive. Look for sunscreen free of para-aminobenzoic acid, or PABA, as the chemical may cause skin problems for children. An SPF of 30 is good.

For lip balm, make sure it has a SPF in it or lips will burn.

SUNDRIES

Insect repellent

Use a natural repellent rather than products containing DEET, which can lead to medical side effects, especially among children. Instead, use citronella, pure vanilla (as opposed to imitation vanilla) or lemon oil of eucalyptus. In each case, the odor repels the insect but is non-toxic for people.

Wet wipes

Pre-moistened towelettes are excellent for cleaning hands and the face, to complement toilet paper, and to help clean cuts, blisters and wounds. To maximize their benefits, get the antibacterial or antiseptic kind. You'll want to carry them in a re-sealable plastic bag. Don't mix the used with the unused ones, though.

Safety whistles

A safety whistle is a very useful tool during emergencies. Its sound will carry farther than a shout, so you'll be easier to locate if lost. A whistle also can be used to communicate with others in your party if they are lost, rush too far ahead, or fall too far behind. It also can be used to scare away some potentially dangerous animals. Carry them around your neck or in an easy to reach pocket so you do not have to dig for them in an emergency. Each child able to use a whistle should carry one.

Space blanket

Also known as an emergency blanket, first-aid blanket, Mylar blanket, thermal blanket or weather blanket, the space blanket is a necessity if you should have to stay the night in the words. Developed for the space program (hence its name), the ultrathin sheet is lightweight and takes up little space. Its materials reflect 97% of all heat, making it an ideal shelter wall, let alone blanket.

Matches
Always carry genuine waterproof matches. If you get lost and must stay the night, fall into icy water, or get caught wet in a downpour, you may need a fire to stay warm and alive. It's not a great idea to transfer regular matches to a waterproof container as you then don't have a strike surface to light them. A cigarette lighter generally is a poor substitute for matches, as they can be unreliable in dampness and can break, spilling the very fluid you need for starting a fire, but it's better than no match. If heading on an extremely long hike into the backcountry with teen-agers, carry a flint and steel kit with cotton and cork for fire. As an alternative, fire starter fuel can be used.

Candle
Bring an unscented votive-sized candle, preferably one that hasn't been used. If you are forced to stay the night in the wilds, matches easily will light a candle, which in turn can be used to start tinder aflame for your campfire.

Re-sealable plastic bags
Quart-size plastic bags normally used in the kitchen will have a number of uses on a hike, from holding garbage and soiled diapers to keeping dry items from paper maps to matches. Always brings a couple of extra bags;

even if never used, they're lightweight and take up little space.

Flashlight

If lost and forced to stay the night in the wilds, a flashlight can come in handy. There's no need to carry anything bulky, though. Micro flashlights with xenon bulbs have a battery life of about eight hours and are more than adequate. Make sure the flashlight is waterproof.

Diapers/toilet paper

Rest assured, if a long drive is required to the trailhead or if heading deep into the backcountry, your children will have to go potty. Pack unused diapers and toilet paper in re-sealable plastic bags so they stay dry. Bring extra bags for the soiled diapers and toilet paper. Wet wipes also may serve you well here. In fact, some hikers don't bring toilet paper but rely on wipes to serve that function. See Chapter 11 for more about children going potty in the wilds.

Toilet trowel or spade

When your diaperless children have to go potty, you'll need something to dig and fill in a cathole. A plastic trowel will work just fine in most soils, but if the surface is rocky or hard, opt for a small metal spade. Again, more on this in Chapter 11.

Optionals

There are several items you don't need to have on a hike, but bringing them certainly can make your trip more enjoyable. Don't take any, though, unless you can physically carry them and only if you plan to use them.

Binoculars

Binoculars are not just nice for getting a closer look at distant animals or geological features, but they also can be used as a navigation tool by helping you get a closer look at where a trail leads. An adult will want a pair that magnifies by the seven or eight power to be of any real benefit. Larger lenses will give you a clearer and more detailed view.

If bringing binoculars, consider also getting small, lightweight versions (with lanyards) for your children. Most will love carrying them around their neck. They won't be able to see as far as you can in yours, but they'll still think seeing a grazing deer or a snow-covered mountain peak "close up" is cool. If children do wear binoculars around their necks, make sure their shirt has a collar so that the lanyard can be tucked behind the fabric. It then won't cut into the skin.

Magnifying glasses

Toddlers to older elementary kids (and even adventurous teens) will enjoy getting close-up looks at everything from bugs to bark, from flower blossoms to the crystalline structure of rocks. As the lens likely will scratch with repeated use, purchase an inexpensive kids version.

Journals and pens

For kids who like to write, nature can be inspiring. If you like to write, you may find that sometimes children are so engrossed in watching ducks swim down a stream or seeing who can throw rocks farther that you'll have time to journal. To keep the load light, don't bring anything larger than a 6x9 notebook, and make sure it has a hard cover, as you won't have a surface to write on in the wilds.

Pocket mirror

A small 2x2 inch pocket mirror can be useful if lost. By reflecting sunlight off it, you can signal aircraft and attract the attention of other hikers on distant trails should you need help. Sometimes a first-aid kit comes with a reflective mirror or a space blanket can be folded to serve the same purpose, however.

Bandana

A bandana can be very useful in a number of ways: sweatband when wrapped around head; earmuffs; bandage; sunshade over neck when wrapped over top of head; washcloth; towel; sling; pad for lifting hot pots. It even can be doused in cold water and worn on the head to keep cool.

Handkerchief

Handkerchiefs are just as useful as bandanas, so long as you don't use them for their intended purpose of blowing one's nose. Wet wipes or some extra tissue paper can be brought along if you or the kids are feeling a little sneezy. The wet wipes and tissues certainly won't be quite as messy as a handkerchief and can be put in a re-sealable plastic bag as garbage.

Bathing suits and towels

If planning to take a swim or to go wading during the hike, you'll want to bring bathing suits, swimming trunks and towels. Wear flip-flops or a shoe (but not the shoes or boots your children hike in) when in the water because sharp rocks or a stick stuck in the mud may sit at the bottom.

Videocamera

Bringing a videocamera, especially a large one, is not a great idea. It adds more weight to your pack and stands a good chance of being broken, not just during a fall but when you set down and lean up against your pack during a rest stop. Instead, carry a digital camera that can take videos. The videos may not be of the highest quality, but it'll save you a lot of headaches and money.

Tarpaulin

When your kids are old enough that you've traded the baby carrier for a backpack, you may want to consider carrying a small tarpaulin with you. These can be useful when building an emergency shelter. They also can provide a barrier between a child and the ground should first aid have to be given or if a bed must be made because an emergency forces you to stay the night.

Nevers

There are a number of items I'd recommend leaving at home: toys, stuffies, hand-held video games, music-playing devices, the kids' mobile phones (or at least they shouldn't be allowed to use them except in the case of an emergency), cigarettes/pipes, purses, and pets (other than dogs) as they'll have to be left in the vehicle and then run the risk of overheating. All of them distract you from nature, potentially create dangerous situations, or can be lost. A lost object means recovering ground to look for it, and if children are involved you'll be the one doing most of the looking.

Parents do differ on many of these objects. Some never would leave the trailhead without ensuring their toddler has some toy in hand. Some believe it's best to let their teenager take his music-playing device rather than get into an argument about it – after all, you got him outdoors, so what's the fuss?

I must admit that I, too, have not followed my advice and let my preschooler take his favorite stuffie on a 10-mile hike through the wilderness. I discussed with him before leaving that he needed to always know where his bunny was and that if he grew tired of carrying it, to give the stuffie to me. He held it the entire way, never dropping it once while riding in the baby carrier. The hike was a great topic of discussion between him and his bunny for the next week.

As a parent, you have to pick your battles.

Sometimes (aka the family dog)

Dogs are part of the family, and kids will want to share the hiking experience with them. In turn, dogs will have a blast on the trail, some larger dogs can be used as Sherpas, and others will defend against threatening animals.

But there is a downside to dogs. Many will chase animals and so run the risk of getting lost or injured. In addition, a doggy bag will have to be carried for dog pooh – yeah, it's natural, but inconsiderate to leave for other hikers to smell and for their kids to step in. In addition, most dogs almost always will lose a battle against a threatening animal, so there's a price to be paid for your safety.

Many places where you'll hike solve the dilemma for you as dogs aren't allowed on their trails. Dogs are verboten on national parks trails but usually permitted on those in national forests. Always check with the park ranger before heading to the trail.

If you can bring a dog, make sure it is well behaved and friendly to others. You don't need your dog biting another hiker while unnecessarily defending its family.

Section III: The Hike

You've picked a trail, decked out the kids in the proper clothes, and purchased all the gear and sundries. Now it's time to put the feet on the ground and head out.

Before doing that, though, you'll want to make sure you have everything needed in the vehicle – and that your children know how to be safe in the wilds. There are a few other things to also consider when arriving at the trailhead.

If you're a novice hiker, some simple rules of the trail exist that you should be aware of, from backpacker etiquette to ways of crossing difficult terrain. And you'll also want to know how to handle problems your children may give you, whether it be dawdling, boredom or a half-dozen other little nuisances.

In this section, we'll look at all of these topics to ensure all of your trails will be happy trails.

Chapter 9: Arriving at Hiking Area

Preparation for the trail doesn't end with selecting a route and buying some gear. The next step is packing. And then you've got to find the trailhead, a more difficult obstacle than maps would lead one to believe it is.

Let's examine what to do during those few hours just before hitting the trail.

Packing

The first challenge is to pack everything you need in either your fanny pack or backpack.

Begin with your water supply. Make sure canteens, water bottles and hydration systems are full; fill them up the night before and leave them in the refrigerator so that you have cold water. Just before hitting the road, strap one canteen to each side of the backpack or fanny pack/utility belt so that they're more balanced.

Next, make a checklist of everything you plan to take. Inspect each item to ensure it is in working order. As you place it in your fanny pack or backpack, mark off the item.

If lugging a backpack, don't place pointy objects near your back or they'll find a way to push into you the entire hike. Generally, the heaviest items go in last, at the bag's top. This will provide you the greatest comfort when walking.

ARRIVING AT HIKING AREA

Packing Checklist

As the following items are placed in your fanny pack or backpack, cross them off (some items may be connected to your belt or backpack, carried around your neck on a lanyard, or worn). You may wish to add items to the list.

- Camera w/ extra batteries
- Candle
- Canteens filled w/ water
- Carabiners
- Compass
- Diapers (if applicable)
- First-aid kit
- Flashlight w/ extra batteries
- GPS (if applicable)
- Insect repellent
- Lip balm
- Maps
- Matches
- Mobile phone
- Multi-purpose tool
- Picnic lunch ingredients (if picnic is planned)
- Prescription medications (if applicable)
- Rain gear (poncho or jacket w/ trousers)
- Re-sealable plastic bags
- Rope
- Safety whistle
- Snacks
- Space blanket
- Sunscreen
- Tarpaulin (if backpack is used)
- Toilet paper
- Toilet trowel

- Wet wipes
- Wristwatch

If an unweaned infant or toddler is with you:
- Bottle w/ nipple
- Milk or formula
- Pacifier

If children are carrying daypacks, place in them:
- Jacket (for rain or wind)
- Maps (duplicates of yours)
- Safety whistle
- Snack

But for some hikers, the packing order is a bit more complicated:

> "In my backpack, the heaviest items always go to the front, which is nearest your back. If the trail is smooth, the heaviest items go to the top. If the trail is rough, the heaviest items go in the bag's middle or halfway up. If the terrain is extremely rugged, the heavy items go to the bottom." – Tim L., Harrisonburg, Va.

Place items you'll need to get to quickly in the backpack's side pockets or at top of the fanny pack. These objects probably will include a first-aid kit, toilet paper and sunscreen lotion. Don't tie lots of stuff to the outside of the backpack as they can snag on branches and come off.

After you've taken care of your gear, do all of the children's daypacks, preferably with their assistance (and if they're old enough to carry a backpack, they're old enough to help). Make sure their pack isn't overloaded. Among the items that should go in it are a safety whistle,

ARRIVING AT HIKING AREA

emergency snack, rain jacket and probably a small first-aid kit. Teenagers can carry more, and you can entrust to their care some of what you used to carry when they were younger.

The final step is loading your vehicle. Most of the gear can be packed the night before, but any pieces involving canteens or water bottles obviously will have to wait until morning.

Get there sanely

Before leaving, always tell someone responsible where you're going and when you expect to return. This will ensure that should you be lost or if a terrible accident occurs that someone soon will come looking for you.

While driving to the trailhead, treat it like any other trip you take with children. Make sure they have their toys, books, movies, music, snack, or whatever else you use to keep them happy during a drive. If you don't, and they have a meltdown or throw a tantrum, don't be surprised if the hike then doesn't go well.

Park safely

When parking, no part of the vehicle should touch a road or the natural area. Other drivers need to get through, and you wouldn't want a wide load or a careless driver to hit your vehicle. You also don't want to needlessly damage the very area that you plan to hike, so don't park on the grass or in what appear to be "weeds." In some places, such parking can net you a ticket.

You may need to pay for parking. Usually it's included in any entry fee or pass to a park. In many places, day use for hiking is free so long as you aren't camping. National forests typically require a pass for day activities; you can buy them either annually (the best deal) or for daily use. They are available at most outdoors and sporting goods stores near the national forest.

Let someone know you've arrived

Presuming you have mobile phone reception, call a responsible party – who already knows where you're hiking – and let them know you have arrived at the trailhead. Remind them again of when you plan to return.

Make sure you stick to this schedule. If you haven't arrived home within an hour after the time you planned and have had no communication with this person since arriving at the trailhead, they should contact authorities (such as the park ranger or local sheriff's office) to report you lost. You also can sign the trail register, if one is available.

Secure the vehicle

Keep valuables, such as CDs, DVDs, purses and videogames out of sight in your vehicle. Most parking areas are safe, but if you notice broken window glass on the ground, then a break-in probably occurred there recently.

Most such break-ins are smash-and-runs, so by forcing the robber to have to look through your vehicle for valuables, you're encouraging him to instead move on to another one.

Take your wallet and some emergency money with you on the hike. Your vehicle is more likely to be broken into than you are to be mugged on the trail.

You want to carry a credit card or some extra money with you in case of an emergency. If one of the kids breaks a leg and ends up in a local hospital, you'll need money at least to buy dinner for your other children.

Emergency information sheet

Leave an emergency information sheet for each person going on the hike. Information on it should include medical conditions, insurance numbers, allergies, blood type, and emergency contact information. If you or one of the children should be injured, this is information that emergency responders, rescuers and medical personnel can use.

You might also leave a hiker's safety form on the dashboard of your vehicle. When rangers pass your vehicle and see it, they'll be able to read it and see if you are late in arriving.

The downside of the safety form is it also lets criminals know how long you'll be gone, giving them ample opportunity to search through your vehicle after breaking in.

But if crime is not an issue at the park or area you're heading into, use the safety form so long as children are with you. Check with rangers or local law enforcement to see if break-ins are a problem where you plan to hike.

Sample Emergency Information Sheet

Child's name _____

Home address _____

_____

Home phone _____

Office phone _____

Person(s) to call in case of emergency:

1. Name _____

   Relationship _____

   Phones: Day _____ Night _____

2. Name _____

   Relationship _____

   Phones: Day _____ Night _____

Physician to call in case of emergency:

Name _____

Phones: Day _____ Night _____

Prescription drugs child is taking and dosages

_____

_____

_____

ARRIVING AT HIKING AREA

Drugs to which child has a known reaction

_____

_____

Blood type _____

Medical conditions_____

_____

Health insurance company name_____

_____

Insurance No._____

Policyholder_____

Sample Hiker's Safety Form

We've gone hiking on the _____Trail

Date _____, 20_____

Time we left the vehicle to start hike _____

We plan to return by _____

Our destination is _____

Names of those on hike are_____

_____

_____

Vehicle make_____

HIKES WITH TYKES

    Model_____

    Color_____

    License plate No._____

    Our cell phone number _____

    Person to call in case of emergency:

        Name_____

        Relationship_____

        Phones: Day _____Night _____

Ready kids for hike

Begin by making sure each of the children is properly dressed. You did this at home, of course, but during the drive kids have a way of removing shoes and shocks and layers of clothing or of leaving their hats and sunglasses in the vehicle.

    Next, apply sunscreen, lip balm and insect repellent to each child. Older elementary school kids probably can do their own (and teenagers certainly can), but you'll need to at least talk younger kids through the steps and make sure they've been thorough. You can put on your sunscreen, lip balm and repellent with the kids. The order that you put on these items doesn't matter.

    Next, distribute the kids their gear, from daypacks to trekking poles. Make sure they put on the gear properly. If you don't, you'll either have to stop along the way and do it or you'll have kids with sore backs, shoulders, necks, wrists or more.

Put on your gear

The time finally has arrived for you to strap on your own gear. That's not so easy to do when you're also trying to watch little ones and making sure they don't discard clothing or gear you just make sure they had.

Double check so you haven't left something valuable in the vehicle that needs to be taken on the trail, such as maps you used to reach the site, your mobile phone, your wallet, and trail mix your kids talked you into munching on early. Once you've done that, get your gear on.

When putting on the backpack, tighten the waist belt snug, then shift the pack as high on your shoulders as you can and tighten the belt again. This will provide better stability when walking and keep most of the weight on your hips rather than your shoulders, which would be tiring.

If you have a baby carrier, put on your fanny pack first, then situate and buckle up the child in the carrier. Next, put on the carrier, grab the trekking pole, and gather the kids around.

Go over safety with kids

It's best to review this in advance before leaving the house – but once at your hiking site, a gentle reminder is a good idea. Through repetition, they'll get it. Even my son at the age of three could tell me after a couple of hiking trips what to do if he saw a snake.

Some ground rules you need to cover include:
- Stay in sight of an adult at all times
- Only drink water we bring in
- What to do if they get lost
- Watch for poison ivy/oak/sumac
- What to do if they see a snake
- Where they should not go (also what not to climb, no stepping into water, stay away from cliff sides and other drop offs, etc.)
- Stay on the trail, no shortcuts

Cover anything else you feel is necessary.

As kids get older and have done several hikes, they probably don't need to go over every item on the list or you can review the rules quite quickly.

Now herd the kids onto the trailhead.

Locate the trailhead

Often the trailhead is a narrow path off of or near the parking lot. The advantage of researching the trail in advance is you'll know where to park and where the trailhead is in relation to your vehicle. But be careful: Sometimes multiple trailheads lead from a parking lot, and signs don't always make clear which trail is which, let alone if it even is a legitimate trail.

To make sure you're on the right trailhead, use your satellite photo of the site. In addition, check it against a key landmark or geological feature on your topo map. Typically the start of any trail is nicely marked by well-placed rocks that outline the path.

ARRIVING AT HIKING AREA

Trailheads usually are well marked, but a multitude of them beginning at a single parking lot or campground can create confusion.

Don't rely on boot prints to point the way. While they are a good sign when walking well-traveled trails, they certainly aren't proof that you're in the right place:

> *"Once while hiking a national forest I found two trailheads at where my map said there should only be one. As there were no signs, I went with the one that had boot prints heading onto it, as the trail I wanted to hike was fairly popular among parents and kids. About a third of a mile on the trail, I realized looking at the landmarks on the horizon that I was heading the wrong direction and fortunately turned around before we got too far."* – Deborah S., Madison, Wis.

Who leads?

As soon as you hit the trailhead, many kids want to run ahead. You let them bound off, excited by their enthusiasm at discovering nature's wonders and knowing that they'll stop along the way to look at something, allowing you to catch up.

Bad idea.

There are too many dangers in the wilds, from rattlesnakes sunning themselves on the trail to missing a turn resulting in them getting lost. It's all right to allow older teens who've done a lot of hiking to take the lead, but preschoolers and elementary age kids simply won't be alert enough to notice all of the dangers. Perhaps they can walk a few feet ahead of you, but they should be keeping your pace – not running ahead – and they always should be in your sight. I often find it's best to walk side by side with my little one. We talk to one another more that way.

Chapter 10: On the Trail

You've taken your first steps on the trailhead and are heading to your destination. It's all downhill from here, right?

Wrong.

Children (and some adults by the looks of a few public campgrounds), need to follow some simple rules of the trail. Knowing how to cross certain difficult terrain also will be to your advantage. You'll also probably notice some funny signs or rock piles on the trail; knowing what they mean will prove helpful in keeping you from getting lost. In this chapter, we'll discuss all of these items that could come up on the trail.

Rules of the trail

Ah, the woods or wide open desert, peaceful and quiet, not a single soul around for miles. Now you and your children can do whatever you want.

Not so fast.

Act like wild animals on a hike, and you'll destroy the very aspects of the wilds that make them so attractive. Act like wild animals, and you're likely to end up back in civilization, specifically an emergency room. And there are other people around. Just as you would wish them to treat you courteously, so you and your children should do the same for them.

Let's cover how to act civilized out on the wilds.

Minimize damage to your surroundings

When in the wilds, follow the maxim of "Leave no trace." Obviously, you shouldn't toss litter on the ground, start rockslides, or pollute water supplies. How much is damage and how much is good-natured exploring is a gray area, of course. Most serious backpackers will say you should never pick up objects, break branches, throw rocks, pick flowers, and so on – the idea is not to disturb the environment at all. Good luck getting a four-year-old to think like that. The good news is a four-year-old won't be able to throw around many rocks or break many branches.

Children from the beginning should be taught to respect nature and to not destroy their environment. While you might overlook a preschooler hurling rocks into a puddle, they can be taught to sniff rather than pick flowers. As they grow older, you can teach them the value of leaving the rock alone. Regardless of age, don't allow children to write on boulders or carve into trees.

Many hikers split over picking berries. To strictly abide by the "minimize damage" principle, you wouldn't pick any berries at all. Kids, however, are likely to find great pleasure in eating blackberries, currants, and thimbleberries as ambling down the trail. Personally, I don't see any probably enjoying a few berries if the long-term payoff is a respect and love for nature. To minimize damage, teach them to only pick berries they can reach from the trail so they don't trample plants or deplete food supplies for animals. They also should only pick what they'll eat.

Collecting is another issue. In national and most state and county parks, taking rocks, flower blossoms and even pine cones is illegal. Picking flowers moves many species, especially if they are rare and native, one step closer to extinction. Archeological ruins are extremely fragile, and even touching them can damage a site.

But on many trails, especially gem trails, collecting is part of the adventure. Use common sense – if the point of the trail is to find materials to collect, such as a gem trail, take judiciously, meaning don't overcollect. Otherwise, leave it there.

Sometimes the trail crosses private property. If so, walking around fields, not through them, always is best or you could damage a farmer's crops.

Pack out what you pack in

Set the example as a parent: Don't litter yourself; whenever stopping, pick up whatever you've dropped; and always require kids to pick up after themselves when they litter. In the spirit of "Leave no trace," try to leave the trail cleaner than you found it, so if you come across litter that's safe to pick up, do so and bring it back to a trash bin in civilization. Given this, you may want to bring a plastic bag to carry out garbage.

Picking up litter doesn't just mean gum and candy wrappers but also some organic materials that take a long time to decompose and aren't likely to be part of the natural environment you're hiking. In particular, these include peanut shells, orange peelings and eggshells.

Burying litter, by the way, isn't viable. Either animals or erosion soon will dig it up, leaving it scattered around the trail and woods.

Stay on the trail
Hiking off trail means potentially damaging fragile growth. Following this rule not only ensures you minimize damage but is also a matter of safety. Off trail is where kids most likely will encounter dangerous animals and poisonous plants. Not being able to see where they're stepping also increases the likelihood of falling and injuring themselves. Leaving the trail also raises the chances of getting lost.

Staying on the trail also means staying out of caves, mines or abandoned structures you may encounter. They are usually dangerous places and wild animals may be living there.

In addition, never let children take a shortcut on a switchback trail. Besides putting them on steep ground upon which they could slip, their impatient act will cause the switchback to erode.

Practice trail etiquette
As with driving on a road or walking on a sidewalk, there are some unwritten "rules" of the trail that help soothe the social fabric.

Let faster-moving parties pass
If hikers are about to overtake you, step aside at a safe spot and let them pass. If you find yourself to be the faster-moving party, don't crowd and push aside the slower hikers but kindly ask them if you can pass.

Don't come to a dead stop in front of other hikers

Hikers behind you will either have to come to a dead stop, too, or crash into you. Both can result in injury. At the very least, it's an annoyance. If you need to stop, pull off to the side of the trail so others can pass.

Be casually friendly

Be friendly to other hikers by acknowledging them as passing and stopping to talk if they so desire. You may be able to share knowledge of the trail.

At the same time, don't give out too much information about yourself to strangers. While most people on trails are safe, you don't want to unnecessarily put yourself at risk, especially if you have children with you.

Don't pet another hiker's dog unless you have permission

Presuming dogs on a hiking trail are safe seems reasonable, but not all are child-friendly. Some friendly ones even may be startled by your child. Kids should stay away from a dog unless it is acting friendly and then not touch unless the other hiker stops and invites the child to pet it.

Walk single file on narrow trails

If you can't walk two abreast on a trail without crashing through branches or going slightly off trail, then walk single file. Widening trails destroys the natural setting and can create problems for other hikers.

For example, a small rock avalanche can occur on switchbacks. Hikers below you won't appreciate that, and the rolling rocks also will erode the trail. In flat grassy areas, a multitude of trails created by hikers trying to walk side by side can create confusion for future hikers as a map only shows one trail through the meadow or prairie.

Know when to be quiet

Keep noise to a minimum and your conversations down when passing campgrounds or other hikers. Many come to the wilds for solitude and to escape the noise and bustle of city life. Respect them just as you would the customs of people in a foreign country when visiting their land.

As Caroline M., of Glens Falls, N.Y., advises:
> *"Shouts and whistles only should be used during emergencies. Turn off your cell phone, too. You went on the hike to be with your kids and enjoy nature, not to chat on the phone."*

Never tamper with signs or other trail markers

Other hikers depend upon these markers so they don't get lost. There are hikers who believe such man-made intrusions scar the landscape, and so they always knock over cairns, or man-made rock piles, when coming across them. I can understand this temptation in remote backcountry, but such behavior on day hiking trails that kids traverse endangers lives.

Always close gates behind you

Some trails cross privately owned land, and through the good graces of that landowner, hikers are allowed to cross it to avoid an extensive detour. If you cross through a gate onto private property, be sure to close it. The gate probably is there to keep pastured animals from wandering onto public lands.

Do not force your way through fences
Besides running the risk of scratching and cutting yourself, it'll only enlarge the hole, rendering the fence useless. The fence is there for a purpose.

Crossing terrain

Though most of the terrain you'll cross with walking kids will be fairly flat, as they age you'll start tackling rougher country. In addition, if carrying an infant or toddler in a carrier, there's no need to limit yourself to flat trails, so long as you know how to traverse slopes, scree and other hindrances. Not knowing how to cross such ground can cause you and your children to fall.

The more you and your kids hike, the easier traversing difficult terrain will become. After a while, it'll become second nature.

Up a slope

When heading up an incline, slow your pace, take short steps, and keep your body upright. This will ensure you keep your balance.

Down a slope

Ironically, going down a slope can be as exhausting as going up one, particularly on a steep trail. Don't let gravity take you down too fast or you'll slip; at best, your feet, ankles and knees will ache by the time you reach bottom. Your trekking pole really can help you stay upright when going downhill. You can maximize your trekking pole's effectiveness by holding it securely with your arms bent at the elbow in a 90 degrees angle in front of you. In addition, test each stone with your pole before stepping on it.

Scree

Scree is small, loose rock often found on slopes, especially in mountainous areas. It can slide beneath your step, causing you to slip, which in turn can cut up your hands as the rocks often are sharp. Walk across scree by stepping sideways so the long side of your feet have more contact with the slope. If climbing up a slope with scree, take small steps with your feet spread-eagled or splayed. This puts your weight on each boot's instep, reducing both strain on your legs and the odds of slipping.

Water

You want to avoid crossing water, but sometimes to reach a destination you'll have to go through small streams, or in the case of a tide or a recent flashflood you may be cut off from your vehicle. With children, it's usually best to avoid a water crossing by properly timing your hike – don't walk a beach at high tide, for example – or simply turning back when the trail ends at a waterway, such as when a bridge is washed out.

If you must cross, do so where the water is calm and no higher than hip deep, which probably will be too deep for young children, meaning you'll need to put them in a baby carrier. You'll typically find calm spots at a bend in the river or stream, mainly because the waterway widens and slows at the turn. Look ahead for any deep water. It will appear dark or greener than the rest of the waterway. Before crossing, check the far bank to make sure it isn't undercut or steep, as climbing out of the water will be difficult for children or for you if they're on your back.

One kind of water crossing you may face is rock hopping across a stream that at worst runs only a few inches deep. Approach any rock hopping cautiously, for the stones will be slippery. You want to keep your feet dry and don't to want to risk falling – children can drown in just three inches of water. First, select your rock, looking for those that are wide enough to support one of your feet and that can be reached with steps rather than jumps. Always test each rock's stability with your trekking pole before committing to it.

If you lose your balance, don't fret about stepping into the water to stay upright. It's almost always better to have one wet foot than to fall.

Waterlogged ground, such as marshland and swamps, ought to be avoided. More than your feet will get wet as you sink into mud, which makes stepping very difficult if not impossible for children. Should children fall, they might land in pockets of deep water. In addition, snakes and insects can abound in such environments.

Trail markers

In most cases, the trail is an obvious path through the wilds. Sometimes, though, there are branching trails not always marked on the map. You can avoid getting lost by following a variety of trail markers. Be forewarned, though, that in some official wilderness areas, man-made improvements are not allowed, so there will be no trail signs.

Signpost

A signpost usually gives the name of the trail and sometimes provides an arrow showing which way the path goes at a fork or junction. Many national parks and forests use a simple wooden pole in the ground that provide such information as the Forest Road number and forbidden activities on the trail, such as driving an ATV over it. Other parks might actually nail a sign to a tree, though this is generally falling into disfavor as animals sometimes chew on the signs.

Directional signs

These signs sometimes tell you the name of your trail, usually at the trailhead, but once out in the wilds more often than not they tell how far another trail or landmark is. They're usually hung at forks or junctures.

Paint blazes

Sometimes shapes will be painted on trees along the trail. Usually a single color is used for the trail's length. Each shape symbolizes a different piece of information.

Cairns

These are piles of stones that indicate you're on a trail. Usually cairns are found in desert areas or on mountains above the tree line.

Rocks and boulders

In deserts where trees are rare, paint blazes may be used on rocks and boulders rather than trees. For environmental and aesthetic reasons, cairns are preferred, however.

ON THE TRAIL

Meanings of Blazes

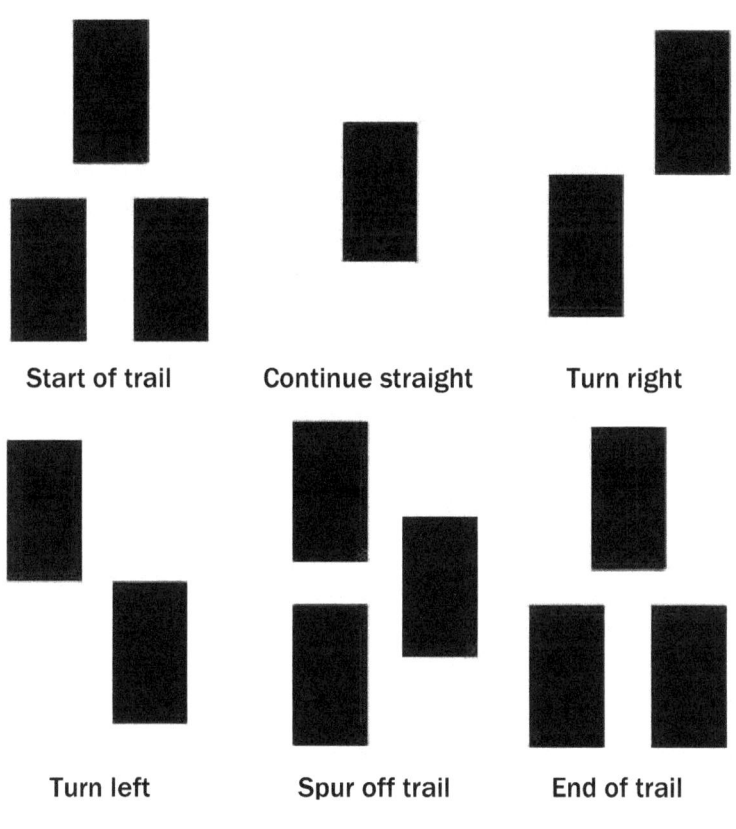

Flags

Surveyor's tape and ribbons of fabric might be tied on trees to indicate an unofficial or temporary trail. This method typically is used during trail construction of a trail.

Turn-back time

When you planned your hike's route, you estimated how long reaching your destination would take. The moment you begin to head back is known as the turn-back time. For safety reasons, you should have a pre-set turn-back time so that you can make it back to the vehicle before dark and so that a responsible person back in civilization knows when to report you missing.

You always should begin heading back to your vehicle at your turn-back time, even if you don't reach your destination – and with children, you may not always make your objective. The turn-back time marks the halfway point of your journey, so walking to your vehicle will take about as much time as did reaching the point you're at.

There are other cases when you'll want to return, regardless of your pre-set turn-back time. If you see a thunderstorm approaching or if fog is beginning to roll in, the time has come to head back. When you reach difficult to cross terrain, such as a water crossing that you had not anticipated, it's better to turn back. If you or your children are tired, shivering or injured, it's definitely time to go home.

Chapter 11: Nuisances

While the trail may be a different place than the living room, kids still will be kids. That means you're going to run into some of the same problems that you do at home – noisiness, sibling rivalry, complaining. In addition, the trail offers its own unique opportunities for behavior problems. In this chapter, we'll examine how to address each of these matters.

Once kids understand the rules of the trail, behavior usually isn't an issue. Typically, there are enough sights along the way to grab their interest, and they'll enjoy the freedom that being in the great outdoors offers. Should they misbehave, though, keep an even temper. You don't want to become a behavioral problem yourself on the trail, or you'll just turn them off to hiking.

Snail's pace

A hike with children won't be done at a steady pace from one point to another, so don't get upset if kids aren't moving as quickly as you'd like. Instead, adopt this philosophy: Always let children set the pace on the trail.

You simply can't force them to go as fast as you. They have smaller legs and can't take as large of steps. Because of that, inclines will be steeper to them than they are to you. Difficult to cross terrain, like rocks or small streams, will be formidable challenges and even barriers to them while you can handle it with a couple of long steps.

In addition, they will stop a lot just to explore and have fun. When kids see a fallen tree, they're more than happy to climb all over it, meaning you are going to have to either pause or tell them to keep going. If what they wish to explore is dangerous, by all means make them keep going, but if it's perfectly safe, then stop and relax. After all, among the reasons for the hike is for your kids to enjoy the great outdoors.

And if that's not enough to slow you down, you'll also need to take frequent rest stops. A 10-15 minute break every half-hour for kids through third grade is about right.

At the same time, watch for the dawdler, or the child who lags behind the rest of the crew even though keeping up shouldn't be a problem. As you can't leave the dawdler behind and don't want to discourage the other kids from having fun, you need to figure out why the child is lagging.

Their daypack could be too heavy, or their feet may hurt because shoes don't fit right. They might feel left out and need a little invitation or attention to regain their spirits. Maybe something is bothering them, and they just need you to talk with them a little about it. A hike sounds like the perfect time to lend your child an ear.

Running ahead

Some kids, excited by the hike and wilds, will run ahead of you out of your sight. That's not a great idea, as it's a good way for the child to let lost or injured.

NUISANCES

When children hit the trails, they sometimes get so excited that they race ahead of the group. Depending on the landscape, this can be very dangerous. Always make sure any child who runs ahead remains in your sight.

You can solve the problem by having the slowest hiker in your group take the lead with the rule that no one else may overtake him or her.

Avoid having fast hikers in front, as it inevitably means the group will become spread out with the slowest hiker exhausted because he's always running to catch up.

Jesse A. of Duluth, Minn., offers another solution:
> *"If you have a large group, split into two parties – a fast group and a slow group. You'll need two adults to make this work, though, as kids never should be allowed in the wilds by themselves. In addition, at the hike's end the fast group will have to wait a little for the slow group to complete its trek, so you may want to have some activities ready to occupy their time.*

Potty time

Kids usually have to go potty at the most inconvenient times. Having the older, potty-trained children go before leaving on the hike can help the cause, but you still should be prepared for them to need to do No. 1 and No. 2 in the wilds.

Bring extra diapers for infants and toddlers. When they go, you'll want to change them right away or they'll get uncomfortable in the baby carrier, leading to a lot of shifting of weight on your back. In addition, during cold weather, a wet diaper can contribute to hypothermia. Following the dictum of "minimize damage to your surroundings," scrape pooh off the diaper and bury it in a cathole. Pack out the diaper, though. You'll find a re-sealable plastic bag useful here.

For older kids, dig catholes. They should be about six inches deep. Cover the hole with dirt when done. Make sure the hole is about a football field's distance from any water source to avoid contaminating it. Pack out toilet paper and wet wipes, otherwise animals will dig them up, leaving trails and woods strewn with feces-covered paper and wipes.

Some children will harbor a fear of such open air toilets. Don't put down the child as a "baby." Talk about their fear and show how no one can see them. Reassure them that you will make sure nothing happens to them and that no one watches. Remind them of those times when they overcame their fears.

Whining

Kids lack the emotional control of adults. The result is they will whine and complain. It's up to you to sort through these complaints and figure out if these are warning signs of bigger problems. All too often a kid isn't really complaining about what's upsetting him. Is he hungry? Cold? Hot? Needs to go potty? Are you going too fast? Do the new shoes hurt his feet? Is he tired? Once you figure out what's bothering him, then you can fix it, and nine times out of ten, all will be fine from there on out.

If your children are whining and look tired, there's no need to keep pushing them onward. It's time to turn back. If your own body is starting to feel sore, you can bet your child already has been suffering quite a bit longer.

Teenagers simply may need to be kidded out of complaining. Be gentle, not critical, though. If your teens can't laugh at themselves, don't push it, or they'll think everyone is picking on them.

Boredom

Kids will get bored more quickly than adults, so if you're bored, there's a good chance they are, too. If they're having a blast and you're not, though, you may want to start hiking like a kid.

When children moan about how bored they are, engage in some group activities. Chapter 12 provides a number of games and other activities that can be done with children on the trail.

If kids are older, allow them to bring a friend. It'll give you more time to spend with the younger children who may accompany you or at least give you more quiet moments to commune with nature.

Here's another clever solution:

> *"Get them to talk about something they really like. This will require a little research on your part, so read up on their favorite video game, movie, rock band or television show, and ask some open-ended question about it. You're likely to get either a long monologue or if there are kids of similar age an impassioned debate about the matter at hand." – Jim M., Eureka, Calif.*

Tantrums

A tantrum is simply the child showing anger and frustration in what for them is a stressful situation. As a parent, you want to first get the child to learn that an angry outburst is not the appropriate way to behave. Given this, treat the tantrum in the wilds exactly as you would at home. This probably means a time out. Once heads are calmer, try to determine what is the source of frustration and resolve it, ideally teaching the children in the process some skill that will help them resolve the problem on their own in the future.

Sibling rivalry

Sibling rivalries generally arise out of competition and jealousy of one another, usually because one child is perceived as getting more attention or a favored status. In the wilds, there can't be anything more than a friendly rivalry. Getting along helps make the experience more pleasant for all, and should an emergency arise, it may be vital for your survival.

While you may not be able to stop the bickering, you certainly can minimize it on the trail. You can begin by trying to prevent the problem from even arising. For example, as a parent don't play favorites or compare children to one another, especially about their hiking skills. Doing so also is a good way to turn off the criticized children to hiking. When children do start arguing, ask each one involved in the conflict to identify why they're upset. Then ask them to each come up with some solutions for resolving the disagreement. If they can't or won't come up with solutions, suggest a few of your own. Have them agree to a solution and follow through. When doing this, be careful to not take sides.

Here's another strategy one parent recommends:
> *"If there's more than one kid on the hike, rotate leaders who will be the point man and set the pace. Agree in advance when the leadership role will change to a sibling."* – Jeff N., Sevierville, Tenn.

Getting dirty

Expect kids to get dirty. It probably means they're having fun. Avoid the problem in part by dressing them in clothes that you don't mind they get dirty. Also, make sure they don't lean against trees with pitch or sap in them during rest stops. To prevent them from spreading their mud and sand to your vehicle, bring a complete change of clothes that they can slip into when the hike is done.

Noisiness

Children naturally will be noisy compared to adults. If they're laughing and talking loudly to one another, they're having a great time, and that's a good thing in the wilds. At the same time, constant shouting and blowing on safety whistles is really irritating – not just for you but for other hikers and campers. You'll then have to remind children to quiet down. A strategy that often works for older children is to talk about their voices in terms of the numbers zero through five. Zero would not be talking at all, one would be whispering, and five would screaming at the top of their lungs when cheering their favorite sports team. When they get a little loud, ask them to "Use voice level No. 3, please." This tells them to tone it down and gives them a reference in their minds for how loud they are.

Risk-takers

Risk-takers are the kind of kids who climb up rocks from which they could readily fall or drown. Risk-taking shouldn't be allowed. If an injury occurs, the hike could then very well be over. Sometimes, rescuing such a child means putting yourself at risk, and that's a very dangerous situation indeed. There's a lot of fun to be had without children deliberately putting themselves in danger.

The best way to deal with a risk-taker is to head him off before he gets to the pass:

> *"Risk-takers are mostly show-offs looking for attention. If your kid has a tendency to do dangerous things and say 'Look at me!' then instead give him some extra attention on the trail and divert his thinking away from doing things to 'impress' you or the other children."* – Robert O., Wheeling, W.Va.

Reluctant kid

There are a couple of different kinds of reluctant kids you might run into. First is the one who doesn't want to go hiking at all, and secondly is the one who doesn't want to explore when there. Each needs to be addressed a little differently.

Doesn't want to hike at all

You'll need to find some ways to get kids enthusiastic about the hike. Consider allowing them to bring a friend along or go hiking with another family that has children (especially of similar age).

You also can involve them in the trip planning, selecting snacks, packing, and navigating with map and compass. Then they feel as if you are giving them attention, and they will associate hiking with your respect and love for them.

Do something special at the destination, so the child has something to look forward to. In fact, this is a great idea even if your child is excited about the hike, as doing something special upon reaching your goal is a great way of bonding. Some hikers carry a small camp stove and whip up cups of hot chocolate for everyone in the party. My son and I always share a package of freeze-dried ice cream while gazing out at the view from the mountain top or rock formation we've reached.

Doesn't want to explore on hike

Let such children focus on what they want to do: scampering over boulders, swimming in a pond, pretending to fight off dragons in the woods. You also might engage them in some activities, particularly ones they like (see the next chapter for some ideas).

Penny J., of Ogden, Utah, offers this unique suggestion:
> "If a kid who is too heavy to carry doesn't want to walk anymore but isn't tired, bribe him by offering him one M&M for every 20 steps he takes. Twenty steps is doable for any kid, especially if there is a reward at the end of it. Be careful, though – you don't want every hike to be an M&M for every 20 steps beginning at the trailhead."

Significant other doesn't enjoy hiking

Hiking almost always is more fun for children – especially those that are young – when both parents do it together with them. Then it becomes a family outing. It'll also be a lot easier for you to keep track of the kids and handle an emergency if another adult comes along

But sometimes your significant other doesn't like to hike (perish the thought!).

It could be the person in question didn't have a good experience hiking as a child (their parents didn't have the opportunity to read this guidebook, after all), or maybe he or she just doesn't like being outside in a setting that's not manicured.

If the former, see if they'll give it a go with you. Ask them not to put down hiking as an activity while on the trail with the promise that if they hate it, you'll never pester them again about it.

One adult going on the hike if your spouse/significant other doesn't want to go certainly is fine. After all, most teachers have class sizes of more than 30 kids, so you with a brood of five or six is (pardon the pun) child's play.

Fear

Generally, if a parent feels safe and comfortable, so will your kids.

Those children experiencing fear in the wilds often don't become frightened until in the woods. Darkness, strange noises, lack of people and heights all may trigger their fears.

To help kids overcome their fear of being in the wilds, pair up so everyone has a "hiking partner." Partners will encourage one another through the rough parts of the hike and watch each other so they don't get hurt. Finally, never push children into doing something they don't want to do, such as climbing a rock, walking along a cliff edge, or wading into water. There's no need to raise their anxiety levels.

Tiredness

Sometimes younger children exhaust themselves by running as soon as they hit the trail. You then end up carrying them most of the way back or quitting the trail early. Encourage them to pace themselves.

Don't hike on days when the child clearly needs sleep. If a child obviously is tired, don't force them on a death march.

Should they tire on the trail, you'll need to carry their gear. Presuming they're young, you might want to place them in the baby carrier for the rest of the trip.

Kids' energy levels also vary from day to day. Maybe last week your child walked three miles with no problem, but today after a half-mile he's dragging. Whenever you notice a sharp decline in energy in your children, it's time to turn around. Tired kids are more likely to wander off, to fall, or otherwise make bad decisions leading to injuries.

Depending on their age and size, they will have to hike back to the vehicle, of course.

Chapter 12: Activities

Infants in baby carriers largely are passive passengers. For my son, that changed sometime during his first year when he began to string words together into sentences and started talking with me. His passivity totally ended when he came down from the carrier sometime during his third year.

Generally, exploring and discovery is enough for kids, but sometimes even they can grow bored with that and become restless. Remember that they naturally have shorter attention spans than adults.

Fortunately, there are lots of tried and true activities you can do on the trail that'll keep kids from getting bored. Most don't require any materials, either. As Tom G. of Boise, Idaho, explains:

> *"Giving kids attention by interacting with them or giving them a goal so they can impress you will do wonders in keeping kids from being unruly or wanting to quit. They can compete in pairs, in teams or on their own, and you can have them switch up or change the activity if it's not quite working."*

Don't bring toys and games from home on the trail, however. You want to keep your load light, and the more that your children bring the greater the chance that objects will get lost, forcing you to spend time looking for them rather than hiking. In any case, the point of the hike is in part to get back to nature. If your children want to play with their toys and games, they didn't need to leave the house to do that.

Nature-related

Each of these activities involves learning about nature and the area in which you are hiking. Ages given for appropriateness are general. Your child may very well be advanced enough to do the activity at a younger age.

I Spy

Name things you see on the trail and have kids point them out to you. List objects that aren't obvious, such as spider webs, dew drops, a crawling bug, or tossing pebbles. Materials: None needed. Ages 3 and up.

Magnifying glass

Pull out a lightweight magnifying glass and look up close at various objects seen, such as flower blossoms, tree bark, pine cones and of course, bugs. Ant hills are great, and if your child isn't squeamish, turn over a fallen log for a plethora of cool bugs. Remember to gently replace the log as it is a habitat for the insects. Materials: Magnifying glass; if you have multiple children on the hike, buy one for each child or pair of kids. Ages 3 and up.

Scavenger hunt

Look for items either using adjectives (find something circular, fuzzy, rough, black, etc.) or make cards in advance.

ACTIVITIES

Make Scavenger Hunt Cards

Kids can create their own fun cards for a scavenger hunt on the trail.

■ **Materials** – Cardboard (such as old cereal boxes), crayons (colored pencils or markers also will do), glue, paper, scissors

■ **Instructions** – (1) Draw lines on a piece of 8x11-1/2 paper so that you have four boxes going across and five boxes going down the page. (2) In each box, draw a different item you might find on your hike: a rock, a squirrel, a tree, a pine cone, a flower, etc. (or paste pictures of the objects). While researching the trail online, perhaps you can show pictures of the path or area to your children to give them ideas of what they might find. (3) Trace the edges of the paper on a piece of cardboard. (4) Cut out the cardboard backing. (5) Glue the paper to the cardboard.

■ **Modify** – You can modify the card to become a bingo rather than scavenger game. You'll need to draw five boxes across rather than four. Mark the very center box as "FREE"

■ **Reminder** – Don't forget pens, pencils or crayons to mark up the card when going on the hike.

Materials: None needed, but if you make cards be sure to bring pens, pencils or crayons to mark them. Ages 3 and up.

Tape collection

Give each kid a piece of duct tape tacked to a piece of cardboard with the sticky side exposed to the elements.

When the kids see something interesting, let them stick it to the duct tape. It keeps kids looking for stuff to put on the tape and makes for a good conversation starter later. Having said this, beware that one of the rules of the trail is to leave things as they are. Still, I can't see any harm in pulling up a single blade of grass or picking an acorn off the trail if the end result is more children growing up to love and respect nature. The key is to not start uprooting whole plants or torturing small animals (like lizards) by sticking them to the tape. Materials: Duct tape. Ages 3 and up.

Rainbows

Using the colors of the rainbow, have children identify something they see along the trail that is a specific color; works best for young elementary-age kids. Materials: None needed. Ages 3-9.

Butterfly net

Once you start seeing butterflies in your yard, consider bringing a butterfly net on the trail. Catching the butterflies is a fun challenge for kids, and if you bring a magnifying glass to look at what you've caught, can make for some literally eye-popping discoveries. Materials: Butterfly net, magnifying glass. Ages 5 and up.

Counting

Working in pairs or as individuals, each team or person counts the number of some object they name in advance – squirrels, dead trees, lizards, oak trees, etc. The object sought should not be extremely common, such as rocks or

ACTIVITIES

ants, so that teams have to keep an eye out for them. Whichever team finds the most of their sought object wins. Materials: None needed. Ages 5 and up.

Finding patterns

Nature is full of patterns, from the shape of flower petals to the coloring of butterfly wings. Have your children identify different shapes and designs they notice on the trail. Materials: None needed. Ages 5 and up.

Grab bag

Have kids collect in a paper bag objects they see on the ground along the trail. At a rest stop, have them exchange bags. They can put their hands into the bag but not look. Using their sense of touch, have them identify the object. Be sure to return the objects to the ground when done. Materials: Paper or plastic bags. Ages 5 and up.

Memory

Discretely collect 10 objects found on the ground – a pine cone, small rock, fallen leaf, etc. – and cover them with a bandana or other material. Uncovering the found objects, give the kids 10 seconds to see them. Cover the objects; the kids have a minute to find as many of them as they can. The child with the most matches wins. Materials: Covering, objects along trail. Ages 5 and up.

Nature bingo

Before going on the hike, have the kids brainstorm about what they might see on the hike: trees, lizards, dragonflies, puddles, pine cones, etc. Have each one make a bingo card with those objects on them (see "How to Make a Scavenger Hunt Card" in this section). When they see each object on the trail, they mark it off on their card. The first one to get a line of words across, down or diagonally, wins. Materials: Bingo cards, pencils (or pen or crayon). Ages 5 and up.

Sniff it

As with grab bag, have kids collect in a bag objects they see on the ground along the trail. At a rest stop, have them exchange bags. They then close their eyes, pull an object from bag, sniff, and try to identify it. Be sure to return the objects to the ground when done. Materials: Paper or plastic bags. Ages 5 and up.

"When you hear" train

Have children line up single file; then pick a sound, such as a bird singing or a snapped twig. When the person in the lead hears it, that person goes to the back. The goal is to not be at the front of the line when the group reaches a certain destination. Works best with a group of young elementary school kids. Materials: None needed. Ages 5 and up.

Who lives here?

When seeing various nests and holes in the ground and trees, try to guess what kind of animal might live there. Hang around long enough, and you may see a lizard, bug or furry critter scamper into or out of it. Don't place hands or sticks into holes, though, to force out the animal. Besides disturbing the animals, this can be very dangerous, leading to bites. Ages: 5 and up.

ACTIVITIES

Usually the wilds' many wonders are enough to keep a child occupied, but if boredom sets in or you want to teach a little about nature, consider playing some games. The activity can be as simple as comparing rocks.

ABCs

Starting with the letter A, identify something on the trail that begins with that letter then move on to the next one. Works best with older elementary age kids who have a broad enough vocabulary to play the game. Materials: None needed. Ages: 8-12.

Senses

Have kids tell what they see, smell, hear and touch. "Taste" usually doesn't count and be careful of kids using "see" exclusively. Encourage their use of the various senses by exposing them to various objects. Crush pine needles in your hand and let them smell it, have them stick their finger into an evergreen's sap, have them hold two very different kinds of but similarly sized rocks and tell you which one is smoother or heavier. Materials: Objects found on the trail. Ages 8 and up.

Signs of wildlife

Have children point out tracks, feathers, fur on fence posts, scat, scratches on trees, nests, burrow holes, etc. Older kids can speculate what animal might have left it there and then give reasons why they suspect that creature. Materials: None needed. Ages 8 and up.

Bark rubbings

If walking through a forest with a variety of trees, have children keep a record of the different kinds they encounter with bark rubbings. Place a piece of paper over each tree and rub an unwrapped crayon sideways over it. Later use a tree identification guide to see what kind of tree it is. You'll need to bring paper and crayons. As an alternative, or in addition to bark, they can make rubbings of leaves that have fallen from the tree. Materials: Crayons, paper. Ages 10 and up.

ACTIVITIES

Be the animal

This is a great game for when some of the group needs to rest but others still have energy. Have the energetic kids get down on knees like a low-lying animal would and tell how their perspective of the world changes (of what they can and cannot see). Then have them climb atop a boulder, pretend they are a bird and again tell about their change in perspective. Materials: None needed. The game can be played by children as young as preschoolers if they simply pretend to be an animal. Ages 10 and up.

Identify animals

Bring a kid-friendly field guide and see how many animals you can identify on the trail; most of the animals you see will be birds and insects, though if in the Southwest, lizards also will be in abundance. This also is best for older kids. Materials: Field guide. Ages 10 and up.

Identify trees and other plants

A kid-friendly field guide can be brought along for older kids. If there is more than one child on the hike, see who can correctly identify the most. Materials: Field guide. Ages 10 and up.

Whichever way the wind blows

If there is a slight breeze, have your children identify which way the wind is blowing. Then have them identify ways that they can determine its direction (the way trees, bushes and grass are bending, the way a piece of paper bends when held up in the air, etc.). Materials: None needed. Ages 10 and up.

Sound map

During a rest stop, have children close their eyes and listen to sounds. Using whatever symbols they like for each sound heard, they then create a map of where those noises are located. After they open their eyes, have them listen for the sounds again. Is the map more "accurate" with their eyes open or shut? Materials: Paper, pencil. Ages 10 and up.

Geocaching

The fun of this game is using GPS and orienteering to find a treasure. Enter "geocaching" into a search engine and find out what the pastime is all about and how to get involved locally. For older kids, it's a great way to turn the hike into a hunt. Materials: GPS, printout of search instructions, an item to add to the treasure. Ages 12 and up.

Identify tracks

Find a kid-friendly field guide or brochure from a local nature center that shows tracks animals make in the region you're hiking. Best for older kids. Materials: Field guide or brochure. Ages 12 and up.

Orienteering

Have kids look at a topo map and identify the real world features: a ridgeline, a draw, a distant mountain peak. With a compass and map, have them track your course on the trail, telling you when you've reached specific points that you've marked on the map. To help kids understand how many steps they need to take to travel a specific distance, they may want to wear a small ped-

ACTIVITIES

ometer. Materials: Topo map and compass brought as navigational tools. Ages 12 and up.

Picture hunt

If you have older elementary school children and each has a digital camera, play a game in which each must snap pictures of as many plants and animals as possible and then correctly identify them. The game assumes that you as the referee and judge you know what the plants and animals are. If the park you visit offers a brochure listing common flora and fauna in the area, that list could serve as a guide – or your children might snap pictures of those listed plants and animals in a sort of scavenger hunt. Materials: Digital cameras, brochure. Ages 12 and up.

Treehugger

After your children have learned to identify some trees, you can play this game to hone their skills. Call out the name of a tree – maple, birch, pine, oak, etc.; the first child to point it out wins that round. Whoever nabs the most rounds out of 10 is the overall winner. Materials: None needed. Ages 12 and up.

Drawing

If your child likes to draw, take a rest stop and let them sketch what they see. This typically works better with teenagers. Materials: Colored pencils, small sketch pad. Ages 14 and up.

Journaling

If your child likes to write, the outdoors can be an inspiring place to put pen to paper. They might keep nature journals, writing about what they've observed on the hike. Materials: Ink pen, journal. Ages 14 and up.

Rock climbing

Definitely for older kids, and it means you'll need to lug some extra gear for safety purposes, as you don't want to fall in the backcountry and then have to spend several hours in pain as being hauled back to civilization for medical attention. Gear you'll need to bring: roping, webbing, carabiners, harnesses, belay devices, climbing shoes. It's not in the scope of this book to explain rock climbing, but there are plenty of good books out there about how to do it safely. Ages: 14 and up.

Birdwatching

Early morning is the best time to watch birds. You'll want to bring binoculars for each member of the party so there aren't antsy kids while waiting to look. Good times to visit a park or nature preserve is when birds may be flying over and stopping over on their annual migrations. A bird identification guide can help you figure out what you're seeing. Materials: Binoculars, bird identification guide. Ages 16 and up.

Kid-tested

These activities don't have much to do with nature, but they're sure-fire winners to keeping kids engaged.

Red light, green light

Kids have to move and stop as you call the signal light color. This is a great way to keep the group together and to play catch up with kids who run ahead. Materials: None needed. Ages 3 and up.

Sing songs
Think of camping songs, driving songs or standards that everyone knows or can quickly learn (such as "This Land is Your Land" or "On Top of Old Smokey"). Materials: None needed. Ages 3 and up.

Simon says
Have kids move in different ways as they head down the trail: long steps, half steps, skipping, sideways steps, hopping, baby steps. Materials: None needed. Ages 3 and up.

Cloud pictures
During a rest stop, lie down on ground or lean against backpacks/trees. Look up at the sky and try to find shapes they can see in the clouds; make up stories about what these different shapes are doing in the sky. Materials needed: Clouds. Ages 4 and up.

One hundred steps
Challenge young elementary school kids (especially those feeling a little down) to see who can take 100 steps first – you or them. Of course, since your steps are longer, if they keep up with you they should win every time. Materials: None needed. Ages 5-10.

Rock hopping
Pretend the ground is lava or a river containing piranhas. To survive, kids have to hop between rocks. This is

only advisable for kids of elementary school age. Rocks must be flat, large, and close enough for kids to maintain their balance. Materials: Patch of rocks. Ages 6-12.

Twenty questions
Give the traditional car and camping game a nature twist. Have the child selecting the object to be guessed select something that could be seen on the trail. Materials: None needed. Ages 8 and up.

Chain story
One kid starts a story, and the others continue it by giving a line or a paragraph. Some story openers: "There was an old troll who lived in a trash can"; "The little girl wiped a tear from her cheek"; "The monster wondered if he'd ever see his home again."; or "One day the teacher told us, 'I must return to my home planet now.'" Materials: None needed. Ages 10 and up.

Find your way back
During a rest stop, blindfold the child with a bandana or handkerchief. Using a zigzagging, indirect route, lead the child to a tree. Have the child touch the tree for a minute. Then lead the child away. Take the blindfold off and have the child find the tree to which they were led. Works best with older elementary school children. Materials: Bandana or handkerchief for blindfold. Ages 10 and up.

Spelling bee
Challenge each other to spell names of objects spotted on the trail. This works best with older elementary school kids. Materials: None needed. Ages 10 and up.

ACTIVITIES

Poetry on the go

With older kids, give the first line of a poem, such as "One day I went on a hike". The next line has to rhyme to with the first, such as "And saw a bear riding a bike." Materials: None needed. Ages 12 and up.

Let them talk ... and talk and talk ...

You just listen, acknowledging what they've said and asking conversational questions to prove you're paying attention and to keep them talking. Materials: Bent ear. All ages.

Section IV: Disasters

While day hiking is fairly safe, accidents and problems can occur. Knowing how to deal with each one usually can avert larger issues.

The best solution to any of these scenarios is to avoid the problem altogether. Before hitting the trail, this means educating children on being safe. On the trail, it means playing it safe, so no horseplay around rocks, water and campfires, which can lead to injuries. Children also should not push or nudge one another on the trail to get past, and you should never press your children into doing something that is unsafe.

It also means keeping a close eye on children:

> *"If there's more than one adult in party, have one take point and hike ahead of the rest of the party, watching for obstacles and dangers and ensuring no one gets ahead of the group. The other adult then can take up the rear and ensure no one lags behind and gets lost or injured."* – Roberta S., Santa Cruz, Calif.

But even the best plans can be laid to waste, so you'll also need to be aware of how to face down each problem. Begin by taking a first-aid course. Besides learning to treat various injuries, a course can teach you how to deal with the stress of an emergency. The Red Cross and many hospitals and clinics offer them at a low cost. In addition, teach your kids basic first aid, or if they're old enough have them take the course, too. It's knowledge that could come in handy far beyond the hiking trail.

Some parent hikers put their small children on a harness or leash when they head into dangerous areas, such as steep cliffs. To me, that feels antithetical to the notion of what hiking in part is all about – the challenge of negotiating the trail, the freedom of the outdoors. If the trail is really so dangerous that a child can't be trusted to be on it, then he belongs in a baby carrier. If the child is too big for a carrier, then the trail is simply too unsafe for him to be on, and the parent shouldn't be taking him there. If you've done your research when selecting a trail, you'll know if a trail is too dangerous or not.

Should a parent hike solo with children? Many longtime hikers say never, as the chances of getting lost increase dramatically. In addition, getting out of the wilds should one become injured makes a sharp decline if solo. Certainly having two adults is better than one when dealing with a group of kids. Having said that, many hikers including myself always take children by ourselves. If you properly prepare for the hike, given the short lengths of the trails you'll hit, the chance of anything going wrong is very low, certainly less than the chance of getting into a car accident, and we drive our vehicles by ourselves or with just our children every day. Further, considering I usually hike in populous Southern California, I'm confident another hiker will be along within a day (and sometimes even a few hours) to provide any help. I wouldn't be so certain if in the backcountry of Alaska or northern Idaho, however.

Chapter 13: Medical Problems

Only go out if there aren't health issues that would prevent enjoyment of the wilds. There's no use in hiking if your child has an ingrown toenail, a toothache or is showing flu-like symptoms. The experience will be miserable for the child and then ultimately for you.

Remember that many of a child's bodily systems aren't fully developed, so their injuries can't always be treated the same way as you would an adults'. Scaling back the amount of medication from adult sizes to "child" portions is both unsound and potentially deadly.

General illnesses

Sometimes a child doesn't begin to exhibit signs of an illness until you're on the trail. Should a child have symptoms of the flu or suffer diarrhea, nausea, vomiting, sore throats or earaches, you'll want to head back home. As the child's body musters resources to fight the ailment, the physical exertion of the hike only will be that more difficult.

Should you as the adult become ill, turn back as well. You're likely going to be tired and have little patience for kid's behavior that you otherwise would let pass. Or you're not going to have the energy to properly watch them to ensure their safety. Toughing it out only invites trouble.

Injuries

Because children lack body fat – or at least healthy ones do – they are more susceptible than adults to a number of injuries, such as hypothermia, frostbite, dehydration, and sunstroke. Because children are still developing, they have difficulty controlling their body temperatures, meaning they will succumb faster to an injury than an adult. Because they're adventurous and still learning the ways of the world, they are more apt to suffer from falls and cuts and bruises than an adult. All of this makes understanding first aid for children a must for adults taking kids on a hike.

Practicing avoidance always is the best approach. If you watch where you're going, your foot won't land on the rake, shooting it in the air so it bonks your nose. But we are talking kids here. Some simply will forget your words of warning and others will not heed your advice. Sometimes you just stumble into bad luck. So you also must know how to treat the injury.

Blisters

A blister is a small, painful pocket of fluid that builds in the upper layers of the skin.

You can avoid blisters by wearing good fitting, broken-in boots and socks that provide cushion and wick moisture from the skin. If certain parts of a foot are prone to blistering, pretreat the area by placing mole skin or an adhesive bandage over it. Long and sharp toenails can lead to rubbing against a shoe and boot and thus blisters on the toes. Always remove tiny stones and twig pieces from a shoe. As soon as your foot or that of your kids' feels any pain, check the foot for a "hot spot," an area of inflammation that is on the verge of becoming a blister.

Always treat a hot spot as soon as you feel it by placing an adhesive bandage over the affected area. While you generally shouldn't pop a blister, do so if hiking. Then clean the blister with antiseptic and dry it to help relieve pressure and to prevent the blister from spreading, which will occur if your keep walking. Place a piece of mole skin over it, secured by an adhesive bandage, so it does not continue to rub against the boot.

As a side note, place a little baby or foot powder in your boot before hiking. While this won't prevent blisters, it'll help reduce moisture on the foot, making the walk more comfortable.

Sunburn

Sunburn occurs when the skin tries to protect itself from exposure to UV rays. The skin turns red and is hot to the touch.

If there's blistering, you have a second-degree burn. Sunburn also can lead to dehydration and sunstroke. While mainly uncomfortable for the child in the short-term, there's also a long-term component of sunburn to consider: The damage due to the sun that results in illnesses such as skin cancers usually occurred during the first two or three decades of life.

Sunburn can be avoided. First, be aware that it generally occurs in open and high altitude areas, even on cloudy days. Sunhats or those with a wide brim to block the UV from hitting the face are a must. Pants and long-

MEDICAL PROBLEMS

sleeved shirts also are effective, but on hot days highly uncomfortable, so you'll want to apply sunscreen.

Sunscreen should be made for children and have a 30 SPF. Apply it to all exposed areas of the skin, particularly the nose, cheeks, tops of ears, and back of the neck, which are more exposed to the sun. Avoid putting it on the hands (which tend to end up in mouths), lips and eyelids. Kids will sweat off the sunscreen, so you'll need to reapply it during the hike. If a rash develops from the sunscreen, seek medical attention immediately.

If your trip includes a swim, get waterproof sunscreen. UV rays can penetrate the water. You'll want to reapply the sunscreen after the kids have dried off. To further avoid sunburn, hike only forested trails during the midday when the sun is most intense (usually between 10 a.m. and 4 p.m.).

In addition, children should use lip balm with an SPF, even if their lips are not chapped. Also encourage kids to wear sunglasses to reduce the chance of cataracts.

To treat sunburn, begin by having children drink a lot of water. This helps replenish the body of its lost fluids, which is an element of being sunburned. Then apply cold compresses or with a handkerchief sponge cold water onto the burned areas. Aloe vera can be applied to reduce the pain.

Wind burn

Wind dries the oily layer of your skin, resulting in a burn. This frequently occurs during winter.

Avoid wind burn first by not getting sunburned, so that means practicing all of the avoidance measures previously mentioned. If sunburned and the wind picks up, cover the sunburned area with clothing, even if you've treated the skin. If walking into the wind, rub moisturizer or petroleum jelly on exposed skin.

If windburn occurs, you'll need to get back that oily protection for your skin. To speed along that process, slather the affected area with a moisturizer that contains an anti-inflammatory, such as aloe vera.

Heat exhaustion/heat stroke

When the body can't stay cool and overheats, people can die. Children are more likely to suffer from over-heating than adults. Because their bodies are smaller, they generate more heat to do the same amount of activity that an adult does. Children also sweat less. Younger kids have a less developed internal heat-regulating system than adults, and more time is needed to acclimate to a hot environment.

Given this, a condition to watch for in children is heat exhaustion. This occurs when blood vessels in the skin dilate, decreasing blood supply to the brain. It sometimes can develop into heatstroke, which is when the body can't cool itself by sweating.

There are a number of ways to avoid heat exhaustion. First, dress children in light-colored, loosely woven clothing. This will help reflect sunlight and allow moisture to evaporate from their bodies. A hat with a wide brim and that breathes also offers protection. Next, start hiking early in the morning if you know the day will be hot. Hiking in temperatures higher than 80 degrees and in the direct sunlight usually is uncomfortable and taxing, particularly as humidity rises. Take more frequent rest stops on hot days. Make sure the break is in a shaded area, where children can take off their hats, as a good portion of our body's heat loss occurs on the head. A water bottle that sprays mist can help keep kids cool when the day gets a little hot.

Signs of heat exhaustion include cramp-like pains, nausea, damp pale skin, dizziness, feeling weak, appearing flushed, rapid heart rate, headache, high body temperature, vomiting, decreased urine output, children denying they are hot when you are, and fainting.

Treating heat exhaustion requires resting children in the shade and giving them lots of fluids, especially water. Loosen their clothing, then sponge or splash the child with water, and fan to increase the cooling rate.

If the child becomes confused or lethargic, he is likely developing heatstroke. Other symptoms of heat stroke include impaired mental function, headache, dizziness, high body temperature, flushed hot skin, and a fast, strong pulse.

In this case, massage extremities to get the blood circulating there then get immediate medical help. If you bring a child to a medical facility, carry them, as a victim should not resume physical activities for some time or a relapse may occur.

Hypothermia

The opposite of heat exhaustion, when a child has hypothermia, the body can't maintain its normal temperature. Our normal body temperature is 98.6 degrees; when it falls just 1.6 degrees, we can start to feel negative effects. If the body drops just 3.6 degrees, it can cease to function.

Hypothermia happens because heat loss from the body occurs faster than the body can keep up, usually when a person is in wet, cold air or clothes.

You can avoid hypothermia by ensuring your children wear adequate clothing and then layered clothing, including a hat, which can decrease heat loss from body. For infants, change diapers immediately, as the wetness can be a source of chill. Also, eat high energy foods on the hike and drink plenty of fluids. When taking rest stops on cooler days, have kids immediately put on their hats and an extra layer of clothing before they get cold, as it will be difficult for their chilled bodies to play catch up.

If a trip into a lake or stream is part of the hike, carry a bathing suit or swimming trunks. Going into water with jeans will mean wet pants, and hypothermia is possible even on a warm day.

Signs of hypothermia include a loss of normal level of consciousness, loss of normal coordination, uncontrollable shivering, and a slow, weak pulse. Victims usually deny they are cold and even become combative about it. That's because their body is confused, so they think they are hot.

To treat for hypothermia, change the victim into dry clothing and snuggle to warm them up. You might cover them with a space blanket. Always seek immediate medical assistance. Handle a victim gently as movement increases the heart rate.

Finally, don't make the error of believing that children can simply keep warm by continuing to walk. By walking, they're actually expending energy needed to keep warm.

MEDICAL PROBLEMS

Dehydration

When one has overexerted himself in extremely hot or dry weather or after great exposure to the sun, the body can suddenly dehydrate.

Though dangerous in itself, dehydration can lead to additional problems, such as heat exhaustion, heatstroke and hypothermia.

Take note: Children will dehydrate more quickly than adults. After all, a glass with a little water in it will evaporate more quickly than a glass with a lot of water. Likewise, children will use up water more quickly than a fullgrown person.

Avoid dehydration by drinking plenty of water. Children need to drink about a quart every two hours of walking and more if the weather is hot, dry or cold and if at a high altitude.

Keep the soft drinks and caffeinated beverages at home. They may temporarily quench thirst, but they won't adequately replace water the body has lost due to physical exertion. Also, let older kids carry their own canteens or use a hydration system. They're then more likely to sip water as they need it.

Here's another idea for getting children to drink their water:

> *"Sometimes kids won't drink warm water. Fill the canteen half way up with water the night before the hike and place it in the freezer. The next morning, fill the canteen with cold water. Several hours will have to pass before the ice melts, ensuring you have cold water the entire hike."* – Rosie M., Durango, Colo.

To avoid dehydration, hiking children should drink a minimum of 2 pints of water an hour.

Thirst is the first sign of dehydration. The less clear (or more yellow) the urine is, the more dehydrated the body is. Other symptoms include nausea, headache, dizziness, muscle cramps and fatigue.

MEDICAL PROBLEMS

To treat dehydration, place the victim in the shade. Use sports drinks or packages of electrolyte additives for kids, not plain water. Don't use salt tablets, as they're difficult to digest.

Drinking bad water

When coming across a crystal clear stream or pond, children often are tempted to drink from it or splash water on their face. Yet, most backwoods streams are full of bacteria guaranteed to give them a bad tummy ache. A major bacteria baddie in drinking water is *Giardia lamblia*, which sickens tens of thousands of people every year in the United States. Fortunately, it's not fatal if you're in good health and get immediate medical attention.

To avoid, only drink water you carry in. You also must limit kids from touching local water; if they get it on their hands or face, it can end up in their mouths. If you must drink local water, there are three options: use water purification tablets, boil it, or use a reverse osmosis filter. The last two solutions probably aren't viable on a day hike. See Chapter 16 for more.

Signs that your children have drunken bad water include stomach cramps, nausea, headaches, and diarrhea. Their body odor also may smell like sulfur. Drinking clean water is the remedy, but ultimately you need to get immediate medical attention.

Eating something they shouldn't

Toddlers like to put things in their mouth, and this can be a problem on the trail: sticks, pebbles, leaves, dirt all could be swallowed.

Advise them not to put anything in their mouth other than the food and water you give them. Be vigilant in watching them.

In most cases, what they put in their mouths will be harmless, but this is where first-aid training comes in handy. For example, you may need to stop them from choking on a pebble or a twig. If they develop any other symptoms, seek immediate medical attention. For more, see the "Berries" and "Mushrooms" sections later in this chapter.

Splinters

Splinters seem mild, but to a kid they hurt. If a child is a third our size, a splinter only a third of an inch long would be the equivalent of shoving an inch-long piece of wood into one of our hands. Yeah, that would hurt. They also can become infected if not treated.

To avoid splinters, don't rub against boards, wood or thorny plants in the wilderness.

Treat the splinter by disinfecting the area around the splinter without touching it. With a tweezers, grasp the splinter as close as possible to the skin and pull it out the way it went in. Squeeze the prickmark so a little fresh blood comes out to help remove any dirt or debris, then disinfect again.

Nosebleeds

Nosebleeds are not uncommon in children from two to 10 years old, and unless it was caused by a major trauma, such as running into a tree, it's probably nothing to worry about. The typical reason for child nosebleeds is picking at it, but in the wilds, warm, dry air and rhinitis brought on by minor allergies to local plants can be a cause.

To prevent nosebleeds from occurring, the child should stop irritating the inside of the nose, such as not blowing it forcefully.

You can treat nosebleeds by having children lean their head slightly forward. Pinch just above the nostrils at the bridge of the nose, applying direct pressure for about 10 minutes. Spit out any blood in the mouth rather than swallowing it. To stop major nosebleeds, apply direct pressure as previously described. If that is ineffective, stuff gauze into the nostrils and seek medical attention. Don't take out the gauze until seeing a medical professsional.

Muscle cramps

Cramps occur when a muscle is repeatedly stressed, usually because it is not receiving enough oxygen. This problem typically occurs during the first portion of the hike. Avoid muscle cramps by exercising regularly so you are fit enough to hike. Whether fit or not, don't overexert yourself by walking too fast. Drink plenty of water but don't overdo it as too much can give you cramps. Breathe slowly and through your nose when walking. Take frequent rest stops as well.

To treat a cramp, stop to rest, stretch and massage the effected muscle, and drink water.

Falls

Fortunately, most falls on the trail are not a big deal. Still, they can lead to everything from a scraped knee to a broken bone.

Children can avoid falls by not running and always watching their step. Usually a fall occurs because a child doesn't see a tree root or a rock on the trail that they then trip over. In addition, don't walk along narrow ledges and be cautious when clambering over boulders lest an arm or the head hit a hard stone on the way down. Don't climb vertically on cliff sides; children easily can lose their grip or loose rock might give way. Climbing is a fun pastime but should be done with the right gear.

Another, more dangerous way falls can occur is when kids enter abandoned mines and wells. Usually mine entrances are boarded up, but even that won't stop inquisitive children from getting inside, so watch them. Mines often have holes or drop-offs in them that can cause serious injury. Children should be told to stay away from mines and wells.

Also, during autumn and early spring, even if there is no snow on the ground, watch your step on bridges or stepping stones over streams and rivers. Ice can form on them. Ice is typically present during the hours immediately after sunrise.

After a fall, always assess the injury's seriousness and treat accordingly.

Bruises

If you have a bruise, then blood vessels under the skin have broken. This could indicate a greater problem, such as a fracture or other internal injury.

To prevent bruises, don't hike under areas where rocks or tree limbs might fall and avoid falling yourself.

MEDICAL PROBLEMS

If you have a bruise, the skin of the affected area will be black and blue, tender, swollen and painful. Reduce swelling by applying a breakable ice pack to the affected area for at least five minutes. Then elevate the bruised area to reduce blood flow to it. If the bruise is extremely large or deep, turn back for the vehicle and get medical attention.

Cuts and wounds

Avoid cuts and wounds by following the same principles of safety to avoid falls. In addition, don't go off-trail through vegetation or climbing on rocks.

To treat a cut or wound, with an antiseptic clean the opening of sand, dirt, gravel and other debris. A cotton swab works well. To irrigate deeper cuts or wounds, a disposable syringe can be used. After drying it, apply an antibiotic ointment and then an adhesive bandage. If a wound, don't use an adhesive bandage but cover it in gauze dressing and get medical attention immediately.

Never apply insect repellent to cuts or wounds (or to irritated skin, for that matter).

Sprains and strains

Sprains occur when a ligament supporting a joint is stretched or torn. Ankles particularly are likely to suffer sprains among hikers. Closely related is a strain, which is when tendons or muscles are torn because they were overstretched.

Avoid sprains and strains by wear hiking boots that provide ankle support.

Symptoms of either a sprain or a strain include pain, tenderness and limited range of motion all in the affected area.

To treat, rest the affected area. If a victim must leave the area, help them walk and carry their backpack for them. Lightly apply the breakable ice pack, or your handkerchief soaked in cold water, over the sprain or strain. Place soft padding, secured with gauze, over the affected area. Elevate the affected area above the heart to reduce swelling and bruising.

Don't have your children try to "walk it off." They won't be able to.

Shock

When the circulatory system fails, the heart and brain are deprived of oxygen, resulting in the life-threatening condition of shock.

Blood loss is the most common cause of shock, but other injuries such as fractures, heat stroke and hypothermia also can lead to it. To prevent shock, adequately treat such injuries.

Even with such treatment, however, there is a chance that shock might occur. Symptoms include a fast but weak pulse, cool skin, chills, pallor, and mental confusion.

To treat, place a tarpaulin or picnic tablecloth on the ground that can keep the child's body off the earth. Lay the child on this covering and raise the feet about 20 inches off the ground. Cover the child in clothing to maintain his body temperature. Keep reassuring the child so they remain calm. Don't let them go asleep and seek immediate medical attention.

MEDICAL PROBLEMS

Dislocation

A dislocation occurs when a bone is wrenched out of its natural position. Typically a finger (especially the thumb), a shoulder, or the jaw are affected. On the hiking trail, a knee or a hip also can become dislocated, especially after a fall, the major cause of dislocations.

To avoid a dislocation, don't fall, make cross-body movements, lift too heavy of objects over one's head, or slam oneself against solid objects, like a boulder. Kids having fun often do these things.

You can tell if someone has dislocated a bone by their contorted limbs, swelling around the affected joint, a pain that worsens with motion, and bruising.

To treat, have the victim support the injured joint, and immobilize it using a bandage or a sling. If the shoulder is dislocated, secure it against the chest using a bandage. Treat the victim for shock and seek medical attention. Do not attempt to reposition the dislocated bone into its socket, as this may cause further injury.

Broken bones

A traumatic injury, the victim will be in severe pain and probably be unable to move the limb. They can quickly go into shock.

Children can avoid breaking bones by following the same safety rules as for falling.

To treat, you may need to straighten the bone. Straightening only should be done when the appendages below the break are blue, cold, numb or paralyzed. Use your handkerchief and gauze bandages to protect any protruding bones. Immobilize the bone by splinting the joint. This will help reduce pain. Next, support the injured bone with a sling or by bandaging it to an unaffected part of the body. Treat for shock. You may have to carry out the victim or call for medical help. If walking out, carry the victim's gear.

Bleeding

Bleeding usually looks worse than it is, but if it isn't stopped, serious problems can arise. In just two minutes, adults can lose enough blood to die, and the time is even shorter for children.

To avoid, following the same safety precautions as for falls and cuts.

To stop bleeding, place the edges of torn skin together while applying direct pressure on the wound. Within a few minutes, usually the blood will clot. Presuming there are no broken bones, lay the person down and raise the affected limb above the heart to limit blood flow to it. Place a sterile gauze pad over the wound and hold it in place by wrapping bandages around the limb. Check to make sure the dressing isn't so tight that it restricts blood flow to the rest of the body; if it does, reapply the dressing. Do not use a tourniquet. Once the bleeding has stopped, remove the gauze bandage and dress the wound in clean bandages. Limit movement of the wounded areas as much as possible and treat for shock.

Scalp wounds can be pesky and usually look worse than they are. Stopping the bleeding will be difficult, but the good news is that very little blood loss usually occurs from such a gash. The child probably will need immediate medical attention to stop the bleeding, however.

MEDICAL PROBLEMS

Altitude sickness

Since air pressure is lower at higher elevations, you will inhale less oxygen in mountainous areas. For most hikers, the problem begins when reaching 8,000 feet above sea level, in which acute mountain sickness can affect both child and adult. More serious and deadlier problems can occur at higher than 12,000 feet, and parents shouldn't take their children above that level. Fortunately, few points in North America are that high, so you'll rarely encounter this issue, unless you're trying to peakbag the United States' or Canada's highest mountains. Children will suffer from altitude sickness more readily than adults. As their bodies are still developing, they simply don't have the ability to adjust as quickly to changes in oxygen levels as do adults.

To avoid altitude sickness, go at a slow pace that allows time for acclimatization. Limit altitude changes to no more than 2000-3000 feet so long as you're returning to your starting point.

Signs of altitude sickness include shortness of breath, dehydration, headache, nausea and dizziness. If the child becomes confused, clumsy, vomits and has a dry cough, the condition is serious. Treating altitude sickness requires descending to a lower elevation where there's more oxygen. In addition, drink extra water to avoid dehydration, and eat light, high-carbohydrate meals. If the condition is serious, get medical attention immediately.

Frostbite

You shouldn't hike in weather cold enough to give kids frostbite. That doesn't mean no hiking during winter, so long as the child is properly clothed. There are winter days, though, when the temperature and wind chill are so low that no amount of bundling up will keep a child warm. In addition, sometimes on days that start pleasant the weather changes unexpectedly, leaving you caught and unprepared in cold weather.

Frostbite occurs when the fluid inside the body's cells freeze. As this fluid freezes, it expands, rupturing and killing the cells. Frostbite starts in extremities – usually the nose, ears, toes, fingers and cheeks – and then moves toward the core of body. As extremities chill, the body automatically restricts blood flow, further lowering the body temperature. Children lose their core temperatures more quickly than do adults, so they will suffer frostbite sooner.

Avoid frostbite by dressing children properly, especially with clothing that will prevent them from getting wet. Don't leave any part of body exposed to cold. Have younger children wear mittens rather than gloves, as this will keep their fingers close together to maintain warmth. Also, take infants and toddlers out of carriers regularly so they can stretch and to ensure good circulation. If children tell you they are cold, take it seriously.

Symptoms of frostbite include reddening skin that eventually turns white then blue or black, a prickling pain in the skin, numbness, and skin feeling hard and waxy.

To treat, get the child to a warm place and remove wet and restrictive clothing. Warm affected areas with body heat, such as placing the child's fingers under armpits or against the stomach. The child's toes can be placed in a hiking partner's armpits. Do not use heating pads, hot

MEDICAL PROBLEMS

water, or stove heat to thaw affected areas as the child probably will not feel if he is being burned. Also, don't rub or massage the affected area as this can damage the skin. After warming, loosely bandage the affected area to protect the skin until feeling returns. If the child needs to walk, do not thaw a frostbitten foot.

Water safety

Kids love water, and incorporating it into a hike is a great way to turn them on to the pastime. Still, water is very dangerous, so you need to make sure children play it safe.

Avoid trails that wind too close to swift-running rivers, and unless the child is a teenager avoid stream crossings. Before being allowed to go in water, children should know how to swim. Enrolling them in a swimming course is a good idea. They also should know what to do if drowning, and older children should know how to rescue others.

If children wade into streams or lakes, make sure the water is clean. Also carry sandals or an extra pair of sneakers as hidden dangers, like sharp rocks and sticks, can be stuck in the bottom of bodies of water and cut bare feet. Don't dive into water where rocks clearly line the bottom or stick above the surface. A head easily could hit the rock, leading to a drowning.

To rescue a drowning child, first you must not panic. More than ever, you need a clear head. All too often, a drowning person pulls down their rescuer or a strong current also grabs hold, causing both to die. Next, you'll need to quickly assess the situation to determine how the child will be saved.

The best of all worlds is when the child is nearby and you can reach out and grab an arm or leg to pull him in. When reaching out, lay down at the water's edge and spread your legs to give yourself more stability.

If the child is out of reach, you might be able to extend your arm via a strong branch or trekking pole. Lay down at the water's edge as previously described and shout to the child to grab the object you're holding out. When the child has a secure grip, pull them in.

Should the child still be out of reach, you may have to get into the water. Be sure that there's something secure for you to hold onto so you don't get pulled under. Extend a leg or arm and shout to the child to grab on. When the child securely latches on, pull them toward you.

You may then need to provide cardiopulmonary resuscitation, or CPR (See the next section on "Unconsciousness").

Unconsciousness

Should a child in your party faint, your ability to reawaken them may very well save their life.

There are any number of reasons why they might lose consciousness, from going into shock to suffering a head injury. By always being safe, you typically can avoid this problem.

Should you suspect your child of being unconscious, speak loudly to him, using his name, as gently shaking his shoulders.

If he does not respond, tilt his head back and remove any obstructions from his mouth. Check to make sure he is breathing.

MEDICAL PROBLEMS

Should he not be, begin the rescue breathing technique. For children, keeping their head tilted and chin lifted, pinch the victim's nose, take a deep breath, and place your mouth over theirs. Give two breaths every three seconds and see if the chest fully rises and falls.

If the victim begins to breathe, continue rescue breaths at rate of 20 per minute, checking for circulation.

Should the child not begin to breathe or stops breathing again, begin cardiopulmonary resuscitation, or CPR. First, find the point on the chest where rib meets the breastbone. Place the middle finger and index finger of one hand there. Put the palm of your second hand next to the two fingers. With one hand only, press the chest down about 1-1/2 inches five times then provide a rescue breath. Continue this cycle of five compressions to one breath until the child begins breathing or you are too exhausted to continue.

Once the child is breathing, place him in a recovery position. This involves rolling him onto his side. Keep the bottom leg extended but bend the top leg at the hip and knee. Their bottom arm should be bent at a right angle with palm facing up. The top arm is bent so that the cheek can rest on the back of the hand.

Immediately seek medical attention by using your mobile phone to call for a rescue, by sending any adults with you for help, or by signaling for help (see Chapter 16 about signaling).

Chapter 14: Dangerous Plants and Animals

Often the greatest danger in the wilds isn't our own clumsiness or foolhardiness but various plants and animals we encounter. The good news is that we mostly have to force the encounter with both flora and fauna. In this chapter, we'll examine how to avoid such brushes and what to do if we still come face to face with the denizens of the wild.

Troublesome plants

Most plants are safe, but a few of them can cause great pain, particularly poison ivy and poison oak. Eating berries and mushrooms you're unfamiliar with also is a no-no.

Poison ivy, poison oak, poison sumac
Touching the leaves of these three plants results in an itchy, painful rash. In the case of poison oak, the irritated skin can blister. Each plant's sticky resin, which causes the reaction, clings to clothing and hair, so though your children may not have "touched" a leaf, once their hand runs against the resin on shirt or jeans, they'll be probably get the rash.

Avoid these three plants unless you enjoy a nerve-wracking itch that can blister: poison oak (left), poison sumac (center), and poison ivy (right).

To avoid touching these plants, you'll need to be able to identify each one. Remember the "Leaves of three, let it be" rule for poison ivy and oak. Besides groups of three leaflets, poison ivy and oak have shiny green leaves that are red in spring and fall. Poison sumac's leaves are not toothed as are non-poisonous sumac, and in autumn their leaves turn scarlet. Be forewarned that even after leaves fall off, poison oak's stems can carry some of the itchy resin.

If children stay on the trail and walk down its middle rather than the edges, they are unlikely to come into contact with this trio of irritating plants. That probably is the best preventative:

> *"Poison ivy barrier creams also can be helpful, but I generally don't like my children to wear them. They only temporarily block the resin, and sometimes kids think they're safe for a long time*

and so don't bother to watch for poison ivy or even tell me that they touched it." – David A., Minneapolis

To treat poison ivy/oak/sumac, wash the part of the body that has touched the plant with poison ivy soap and cold water. This will erode the oily resin, so it'll be easier to rinse off. If you don't have any of this special soap, plain soap sometimes will work if used within a half-hour of touching the plant. Apply a poison ivy cream and get medical attention immediately. Wearing gloves, remove any clothing (including shoes) that has touched the plants, washing them and the worn gloves right away.

Stinging nettles

Fortunately, nettles only result in the temporary pain of being stung. Watch for an itchy red rash, however, as this indicates an allergic reaction. To avoid nettles, stay in the middle of the trail. In addition, if walking through an area with nettles, cover exposed parts of body with clothing.

Treat a nettle cut by plastering baking soda or a cold compress on the area that stings. If an allergic reaction occurs, seek medical attention.

Berries

Certainly the pleasure of some hikes is tasting the ripe, natural berries found along the trail. Before eating any berries, though, children should ask you if it's okay to do so. That means you'll need to familiarize yourself with differing berries to give the right answer. If you don't know the answer, it's best to never eat any found on the trail.

Some Poisonous Berries
Never eat berries from these plants:
- Castor oil
- Daphne
- English ivy
- Holly
- Lantana
- Mistletoe
- Nightshade
- Virginia creeper
- Yew

That won't stop a few overly inquisitive kids from sampling a few when you're not looking, of course.

The symptoms of poisoning from berries differ with each type, but generally nausea, vomiting and diarrhea will result. Blurred vision, drowsiness, dilated pupils, difficulty breathing, and an accelerated heart rate also can occur. Shock is a distinct possibility.

If your child eats potentially poisonous berries, treat for shock if necessary and seek medical attention immediately. Do not induce vomiting, as sometimes this may be more harmful than beneficial. Also, try to identify which berries were eaten to help doctors with a diagnosis.

Mushrooms

Never eat or even touch a mushroom unless you are absolutely sure that it is safe. Children have a way of getting their fingers into their mouths, and if it is a poisonous shroom, that's bad news. The symptoms and treatment are the same as for eating poisonous berries.

Thorns and burrs

These plants typically are more an annoyance than anything, but with a child the nuisance can be enough to put an end to the hike. If left untreated, infections also can result.

The plants can be avoided by walking down the center of the trail.

Use tweezers to pull out thorns. Then swab the site with an antiseptic such as iodine.

Cockleburs, nature's original version of Velcro, simply need to be pulled them off. Be aware that they can prick you as you're doing that, so you may want to wear thick gloves.

Animal attacks

If you're fearful of running into wild animals on the trail, rest easy as you probably won't. In fact, you'll probably see very little wildlife other than birds, squirrels, lizards and the occasional bug. If you do see a wild animal of any size – deer, fox, coyote – it certainly will be the highlight of your hike. Still, there's always the possibility that you'll stumble across a potentially dangerous animal.

A strategy of avoidance is best. Don't be tempted to feed wild animals. Besides inviting an aggressive attack on you, it teaches animals that humans are a source of food, meaning some are less likely to hunt or graze on their own but instead become a nuisance and even a threat to people. Such is the case with many national parks bears, who've learned to raid dumpsters and tents and even break into vehicles for food. Also, don't pick up animals, as their

MEDICAL PROBLEMS

natural inclination is to bite and claw when held. It's not cute to have a child get close to a wild animal for a picture when the creature bites or mauls them.

Snakes

Some snakes, such as the cottonmouth or water moccasin in the Southeast and the diamondback rattlesnake in the Southwest, are extremely venomous, killing within an hour of a bite. Fortunately, poisonous snakes don't always inject venom when they bite, and some only spew a small amount that is survivable.

You can avoid snakes by staying out of tall grass. Don't stick hands into dark holes and rocky crevices, don't turn over rocks, and don't hike at dusk or night when many snakes hunt. While climbing rocks, be careful where you stick your hand as a snake may be sunning itself.

If you see a snake, slowly back away from it. If you hear a rattle, stand still. In both cases, the snake usually will scoot away. Don't try to get a closer look, as it invites attack, especially from a rattler, because it then feels cornered. A snake can strike at about a third of its body length, so you'll probably be just far enough away that it can't attack. Also, don't mess with baby snakes for they too will bite.

Carry a snake bite kit if you walk through an area that has a high count of poisonous snakes. First learn how to use it before heading into the wilds, though. You can do more harm than good if you misuse the kit, which usually involves suctioning the venom from the bite area.

Sometimes hikers walking through grass don't even realize they've been bitten (this is why staying on the clear trail is vital), and sometimes you stumble a little too close to a snake. Symptoms include pain and burning at the bite site followed by swelling and blistering. Nausea and vomiting, with numbness and tingling about the mouth, fingers and scalp also are indications. If the bite is severe, the victim also will grow faint and dizzy and have a weak pulse and cold, clammy skin. They may go into shock.

To treat a snake bite, lay the child down and reassure him to control his panic. Place a light compression bandage above the bite, as this can slow the spread of venom. Do not use a tourniquet, however. Then call for help and seek medical attention immediately.

Finally, if at all possible try to identify the snake so the right anti-venom can be used when the victim receives medical treatment.

Bug bites and stings

The dangers of bug bites and stings range from just a minor annoyance to life-threatening diseases. In addition, once bitten, children tend to scratch the spot, resulting in a higher rate of infection than in adults.

You can avoid insects first and foremost by staying out of areas where they breed, such as swamps and bodies of still water. In mountainous areas, insect season usually occurs about two weeks after snow melts, so avoid hiking at that time.

Remember that what attracts bugs are scents, so skip the perfume, aftershave, lotions and hairspray when hiking. Scented disposable diapers also can attract bugs.

Mosquito netting and insect-proof head nettings are effective at warding off bugs, but if you have to hike through areas necessitating that level of protection, it's probably not a great place to take kids.

Insect repellent also works – and is recommended – though there is much to consider before putting it on.

First, don't swab one- or two-month-old infants with any kind of insect repellent. For all other children, avoid those repellents containing DEET or picaridin and instead choose a product made with oil of lemon eucalyptus, which works just as well but doesn't carry any potential side effects.

Test whatever repellants you purchase before heading into the wilds (especially if you do buy a repellent containing low concentrations of DEET and picaridin, which reportedly are safe). You don't want your child to have an allergic reaction in the woods with a long walk out and then a long drive to an emergency room.

When putting repellent on children, don't spray directly onto their face as it likely will get into their eyes, mouth and nostrils. Instead, spray on your hands and apply it. Do not place repellent on eyes, eyelids, lips, mouths, hands, cuts or wounds, and use it sparingly around the ears. With young children through early elementary school, you should apply it yourself. If a child develops a rash or has an allergic reaction to the repellent, wash it off immediately and get medical attention.

To treat any bug bite, clean the site with soap and water and apply an anti-itch cream, hydrocortisone, or Neosporin with Lydocain. Encourage kids not to itch the bite. On young children, cover the bite or sting with an adhesive bandage so they don't scratch it open.

Whether bit or not, when you get home, wash off with soap and water areas of the body where repellent was applied. Also launder any clothes that came into contact with repellent.

Bees, hornets, wasps and yellow jackets

Though most bee stings aren't deadly, they should be taken seriously. Stings can lead to anaphylactic shock and death. To avoid being stung, stay away from areas where bees, hornets, wasps and yellow jackets might live. Even if no hive is in sight, you usually can determine their home by watching where they disappear – behind a bush's or tree's leafy branches, crawling into a ground hole, or a hollow log opening.

If one flies near your children, they shouldn't swat at it or run. This may anger the insect into stinging. Instead, remain calm and let it fly away. If it lands on your children, have them brush it off and calmly walk away.

Remove the honeybee stinger by scraping it out with a fingernail (bumblebees, hornets and wasps don't leave a stinger and can sting repeatedly). Don't use tweezers on the honeybee stinger as this may release more venom into the skin. Carry oral Benadryl to slow allergic reactions. However, if a severe reaction occurs – such as a bad swelling and rash in areas where the sting didn't occur, especially on the eyes and mouth – seek medical attention immediately. If the child is allergic to bee and wasp stings, be sure to carry prescribed medications to treat it. A cold compress can be placed on the spot to reduce minor swelling.

Mosquitoes

Their burning bites are more of a nuisance than anything, but mosquitoes can carry deadly diseases, such as West Nile virus.

To avoid mosquito bites, stay away from water at dusk and early evening when they tend to come out. You also can wear hats with flaps and tie a loose bandana around the neck to keep the pesky little critters away. Don't hike in areas heavily infested with mosquitoes, such as near old tire dumps that can hold sitting water and thus are the bug's breeding grounds. Finally, if you see a swarm of mosquitoes, expect there to be more swarms and move away.

Treat a mosquito bite as you would a typical bug bite: wash with soap and water, apply an anti-itch cream, hydrocortisone or Neosporin with Lydocain, and don't itch.

Ticks

Ticks can infect people with Lyme disease and Rocky Mountain spotted fever.

They usually leap onto people from the top of a grass blade as you brush against it, so walking in the middle of the trail away from high plants is a good idea. Wearing a hat, a long sleeve shirt tucked into pants, and pants tucked into shoes or socks, also will keep ticks off you, though this is not foolproof as they sometimes can hook onto clothing. A tightly woven cloth provides the best protection, however. Children can pick up a tick that has hitchhiked onto the family dog, so outfit Rover and Queenie with a tick-repelling collar.

If heading into an area where ticks live, after the hike you'll want to examine your children's bodies for them. Check warm, moist areas of the skin, such as under the arms, the groin and head hair. If they wear light-colored clothing, the tiny tick will be easier to spot.

Also check children for signs of disease from ticks. Look for bulls-eye rings, a sign of a Lyme disease. Other symptoms include a large red rash, joint pain, and flu-like symptoms. Indications of Rocky Mountain spotted fever include headache, fever, severe muscle aches, and a spotty rash first on palms and feet soles that spread, all beginning about two days after the bite.

To get rid of a tick that has bitten your child, drip either disinfectant or rubbing alcohol on the bug, so it will loosen its grip. Grip the tick close to its head, slowly pulling it away from the skin. This hopefully will prevent it from releasing saliva that spreads disease. Rather than kill the tick, keep it in a plastic bag so that medical professionals can analyze it should disease symptoms appear. Next, wash the bite area with soap and water then apply antiseptic.

If any of the previously mentioned symptoms appear, seek medical attention immediately. Fortunately, antibiotics exist to cure most tick-related diseases.

Chiggers

Chiggers leave an itchy red bump followed by red welts that are even more maddeningly itchy. There's no real threat of disease or infection, though.

Unfortunately, chiggers are so small they can't be seen by the unaided eye. To keep them off you, apply insect repellent to ankles, the waist and wrists. Sublimed sulfur is particularly effective (be forewarned that sulfur will make you smell quite unpleasant). Wear tightly woven clothes, long-sleeve shirts buttoned tightly at the wrist, pants rather than shorts, high shoes or boots, and tuck pants into the boots. Avoid going into low, damp areas where chiggers reside, especially on warm afternoons, as chiggers are active when the ground temperature is between 77 degrees and 86 degrees. Stay to the center of the trail as chiggers usually reside in tall grass and brush. Wash your clothes as soon as you get home as chiggers can linger on fabric and bite you later.

There is no cure for a chigger bite other than time. Lotions can reduce the itching somewhat but applying a local anesthetic such as Benzocaine is effective for several hours.

Spiders

As with mosquitoes, the bite from the spider is mostly just a nuisance. Still, allergic reactions can occur, and a few spiders are downright deadly. The most dangerous spiders are various widows, the brown recluse and tarantulas.

To avoid spider bites, don't stick hands into dark holes or rocky crevices and don't turn over rocks. Spiders live in such areas and may bite if surprised and think they're under attack.

Treat a spider bite by washing the bite area with soap and water. A cold compress can help alleviate the swelling and redness. Diphenhydramine tablets can be taken to reduce the itch while acetaminophen will help relieve severe pain. If a severe reaction occurs or you know the bite was from a poisonous spider, seek immediate medical treatment.

A few don'ts ... Aspirin won't reduce the inflammation of a spider bite and shouldn't be taken by children. Don't bother with antibiotics, as they're not designed for treating spider bites. Finally, don't cut open the bite mark as it may lead to infection.

Scorpions

Fortunately, in North America only two varieties of scorpions are deadly, and both live in the Arizona desert. Even if not dangerous, a scorpion's sting will be painful.

You can avoid a scorpion sting by not sticking hands into dark holes and rocky crevices and not turning over rocks, all of which could be homes for these little arthropods.

If stung, you'll feel instant pain or burning, numbness and tingling, and the bitten area will be sensitive to touch.

Treatment includes washing the stung area with soap and water then applying a cold compress it. You also should elevate a stung limb above heart level. Always bring a young child stung by a scorpion to the emergency room. For older teens, if reactions in addition to those previously listed appear, then bring them as well to the ER.

Other creepy crawlies

There are plenty of other bugs you might encounter on the trail, most of which are harmless, though children might find them frightening or at least bothersome:

MEDICAL PROBLEMS

- **Ants** – Their bites can leave a sting, and their crawling all about you also can be annoying. Avoid them by being careful not to toss your gear on an ant hill or by sitting against a tree with sap, which ants may feed upon.
- **No-see-ums** – These tiny biting flies live near water and sometimes fly in swarms. You can avoid them by wearing insect repellent and moving away from swarms. Their bites are innocuous beyond the itch and the sometimes 1-2 inch red swelling. Don't scratch the swelling or it could become infected.
- **Horseflies** – Generally the bite is harmless, but it can be painful. Clean the bite area with soap and water. A topical hydrocortisone cream usually will reduce both the swelling and itching. Liquid antihistamine (or for adults, a tablet) also can help.
- **Gnats** – Gnat bites are benign as well, minus the itching and swelling. Use calamine lotion to soothe the itching and don't scratch it.

Other animals

Injuries from other animals are rare but do occur. To avoid becoming one of those statistical oddities, keep your distance. Never feed or approach wildlife. Even if docile, the animal may bite when you get close to it. If it is sick, and a bite occurs, the child could contract a disease. If there are reports in an area of dangerous animals attacking people, don't hike there.

Bears

Black bears appear all over North America and the rarer grizzly in remote areas of the West. You can avoid them by staying out of bear areas in spring when they're awaking from hibernation or tending cubs. Typically bears will avoid us, but a mother who thinks her cubs are threatened more than likely will chase if not attack you. If you stumble across a bear with cubs, keep your distance and move away from them. Sometimes the mother will send her cubs up a tree as she watches to see if you are a threat; don't pass between her and that tree, or she'll attack.

Also, avoid berry patches in fall. If you notice signs of bears, like paw prints, droppings, demolished berry bushes, claw marks on trees or the smell of carrion, you shouldn't continue onward.

Avoidance always is a better solution than being forced into a situation where you have to scare off an attacking bear:

> *"Some hikers recommend jingling bells, but if you're that close to a bear that you need to do so, you probably won't have enough time to get the bells from your backpack should it decide to attack. You also can throw rocks at the bear if it approaches, but this probably necessitates that you bend down, making you an easier target for a fast-moving animal. Pepper spray will ward off a bear, but often by the time the danger is upon you, again you won't be able to reach for the spray or you'll end up spraying it so some will go on you, meaning you suffer much the same fate as the bear (which is slightly better, I suppose, than being at the bear's mercy)."* – Eric M., Bend, Ore.

If you do encounter a lone bear, don't turn your back to it but gather everyone in the group together in a single cluster, make as much noise as possible, and move slowly in opposite direction. Bears usually won't attack a group of more than four people.

If attacked, don't run but play dead by lying on the ground, bringing your legs to your chest, tucking in your head, and covering the back of your neck with your hands. The bear might swat and sniff at you, but when it sees you're playing dead, it won't consider you a threat.

Mountain lions

Usually cougars don't want to be seen and will remain hidden, but there are stories of hungry lions that have attacked humans.

Watch for signs of cougars, like paw prints, droppings, claw marks on trees or the smell of carrion. If you see any of these indications, turn back.

If you encounter a cougar, as with bears don't turn your back to it but keep your space and give it time to retreat. Gather your group into a single cluster and get noisy. If the cougar approaches, wave you trekking poles and shout. You want to appear big to intimidate it, so don't crouch, bend over or down to pick up children, or run. All of those moves make you look smaller. If children are about to panic and run, though, then it's usually smarter to grab them.

If a cougar does attack, fight back in any way you can. Remember that the lion almost certainly will be stronger and faster than you. Try to protect your neck and head when doing so (in short, good luck).

Skunks

Skunks can carry rabies, but the greatest danger is that they'll spray you with a scent that lingers for days.

Stay away from areas where skunks might live or hang out, such as brush piles and beneath fruit trees. If you smell a skunk, move away from the area. If you see one, back away slowly.

Should you be sprayed, mix 1 quart of hydrogen peroxide, a 1/4 cup baking soda and 1 teaspoon of liquid hand soap in a bucket. Starting at the crown of the head, pour the mixture onto the sprayed child and rub it into the skin (including where there's hair). Don't get it in the eyes, mouth or nose, though.

Dispose of the sprayed clothes, as the scent can't be laundered out.

Wolves and coyotes

Wolves really aren't a danger to hikers. They are highly reclusive and being endangered you are very unlikely to ever encounter them unless heading deep into the backcountry.

Coyote attacks also are rare except in built-up areas where their habitat has been wiped out. Should you see a coyote in the wilds, don't try to get any closer. Don't run either, especially if a child, since that may invite an aggressive coyote to strike. Should it attack, yell at it. If bitten by a coyote, get immediate medical attention.

Hoofed animals

Deer, elk, moose and bison actually kill more people annually in North America than do bears and mountain

MEDICAL PROBLEMS

lions. Usually the problem is people who mistakenly think that herbivores can't be dangerous and provoke the beasts by getting too close or by cornering them. This is an issue especially if the hoofed animal has young nearby. Their antlers and horns, not to mention their hooves, can be quite lethal.

You can avoid the danger simply by keeping your distance. Don't try to feed them or get close for a snapshot. Once you see an agitated animal – especially one that's pawing its hooves at the ground and huffing as staring at you – back off.

Newborns

Sometimes you'll stumble across newborn fawns, fox cubs or other babies in the wilds. Stay away from them. Newborns can bite just as well adults – or worse, the mother may be nearby and become very agitated by your interest. In addition, the newborn may be ill, which could result in your children picking up the disease. Also, sometimes mothers will not return to their newborns if humans stay around too long, as can be the case with white-tailed deer.

Rabid animals

Rabies affects the nervous system and can be fatal. Raccoons, foxes, coyotes and skunks all are common carriers. They can spread it to humans by biting us.

You can avoid rabies by not trying to feed wild animals, which invites bites. Also, stay away from animals that show signs of having rabies; for example, if you see a nocturnal animal wandering around during daylight hours (and the list of common carriers above are mainly nocturnal), rabies is a distinct possibility for their behavior. Other signs of rabies are animals that are unsteady on their feet, that have lost their natural fear of man, or that behave oddly. If bitten by a rabid animal (or any animal for that matter), get immediate medical attention.

Trapped animals

Despite your desire to show mercy, don't go near a trapped animal. It probably will bite. The trap also may injure you as you try to free the animal. Should you see a trapped animal – or traps of any kind on public lands – immediately report it to the park ranger or authorities. The trap probably has been illegally set.

Livestock

You may need to cross private land during the hike, and it's quite possible you'll encounter livestock along the way. Don't presume that domesticated animals will be docile. Give them their space just as you would a wild animal. You should never startle cattle or sheep, as they easily can break into a stampede. Stay out of the way of bulls, as they will protect their herd.

Upon returning to your vehicle, always report aggressive animals to authorities. Bears and mountain lions may have to be removed from the area to prevent attacks on humans.

Chapter 15: Bad Weather

If you've done your research right, storms shouldn't be an issue because you'll only hike on sunny, fair weather days. But freak storms can blow in from the ocean, and in the mountains microweather systems can surprise you, especially when moving between elevation levels.

Lightning

Lightning provides a spectacular show for free, but it's also potentially quite deadly.

Once you hear thunder, lightning is not far off. Thunder is the traveling ripple caused by lightning's shock wave as it darts through the sky.

Rain need not be falling for lightning to hit you. An electrical storm is a major cause of lightning strikes.

To avoid lightning, you want to get away from places where it is most likely to strike: above the tree line on mountains; the mouth of a cave; a solitary tree; depressions; and ledges or wet ground.

If on a mountain, immediately descend to below the tree line. A thick tree grove is the best form of natural shelter. Remove metal from your body and sit on your backpack to keep you separated from the ground. Crouch as low as you can, shielding your head with your arms.

Downpours

Rainstorms, especially those with lightning, can be dangerous. Avoid them by immediately returning to your vehicle once storm clouds form, lightning is spotted, or thunder is heard. You want everyone to stay dry, especially if you're carrying an infant or toddler.

Clouds do not necessarily mean rain. Storms are brewing when clouds darken and rise vertically into an anvil shape.

If caught in heavy rain, put on a poncho, head for a low spot or thinly wooded area, and stay low until it passes. Stay away from high ground, depressions where puddles can form, and trees or other tall objects that attract lightning. Never stand in a dry riverbed or wash during a thunderstorm. Floodwater could crash toward you and easily sweep away smaller children.

Flashfloods

Downpours several miles away can quickly fill sandy washes near where you're hiking with fast-moving water as the rain flows into the intermittent stream. Streams flowing off mountains also can quickly flood from rain at higher altitudes while the mountain base sees no precipitation.

Don't hike through and never rest in sandy washes unless you're certain that no rain is forecast for about 100 miles distant. If you see water levels rising or the current picking up in a stream or river, immediately seek higher ground.

Tornadoes

Tornadoes form quickly, usually in areas about to experience severe thunderstorms. By leaving an area to avoid a thunderstorm, you should be able to avoid a tornado.

If one is approaching you, seek shelter in a ravine or a cave. If on flat ground, find the lowest depression or ditch possible.

And never make this mistake:

"Don't seek shelter beneath concrete bridges of highway underpasses. The underpass can act as a wind tunnel during a tornado. Debris will fly right at you at super-high speeds" – Josh S., San Antonio, Texas

Snowstorms

Getting stranded in a snowstorm means at best you'll only have days to live unless soon rescued. Hypothermia, frostbite, lack of water due to it freezing and the inability to forage for food or to find tinder and branches to make a fire all make survival extremely difficult.

If you've planned your trip correctly, you shouldn't be in the wilds when a snowstorm is forecast. Mountain weather is highly changeable, however, and it's quite possible in late spring and early autumn for one to surprise you at a high elevation. As soon as you see any signs of clouding over, feel a significant drop in temperature, or notice high winds or snowflakes, immediately descend to a lower elevation.

If walking is no longer viable – snow can hide the trail and bring visibility to zero – immediately construct a shelter to diminish the affect of wind and wet snow. Huddle together for warmth. Do not eat snow or suck on ice as it will lower your core body temperature. Immediately call for help, and don't send anyone for help as they easily can get lost in the snowstorm.

Fog

Banks of fog can quickly roll in on mountains and coastlines, making travel difficult and disorienting. Fog will obscure landmarks that help you navigate and the very sights that motivated you to hike the route. It is wet, generally cold, and even can be windy, quickly lowering enthusiasm and potentially resulting in hypothermia.

This is where having GPS is particularly beneficial in navigation. Make sure the group stays close together and return to the vehicle as quickly as possible.

Chapter 16: Stuck in the Wilds

The worst case scenario for a day hiker is getting stuck in the wilds for a night with no way out. This usually happens because the hiker is lost, injured or cut off by some natural calamity like a flashflood or forest fire.

Given this, the best way to avoid such a crisis is to ensure you navigate the trail correctly, that everyone plays it safe, and that you stay out of or leave the wilds on days when the weather turns bad. All of that is easier said than done, of course.

The good news is the chances of you ever having to stay a night or two in the wilds while awaiting rescue are extremely low:

> *"Despite years of going day hiking, including getting lost once and peakbagging a mountain on the day a devastating fire began in the same forest, I've never had to go into survival mode and spend a night wondering if it would be the last either my children or I were alive. By being safe and immediately returning to our vehicle when weather looked bad, we've always made it back home well in time for dinner."* – Marc S., Lakeport, Calif.

Marc S. is right: By playing it safe, you'll almost always avoid an even more threatening situation. At the same time, strange events can conspire against you, leaving you stuck in the wilds despite your best efforts. In such instances, you'll need to know how to survive until rescuers reach you.

Forest fires

With global warming and current land management practices in national forests and parks, the threat of forest fires continues to grow, particularly in the West. Do not hike through any area where a forest fire is occurring, especially to "see" the fire. Besides being dangerous, it will be an unpleasant experience as you find smoke choking you.

Sometimes fires begin while you're already on the trail. If you see or smell smoke (and it's clearly not just a campfire), immediately return to your vehicle – presuming the fire isn't between you and it – and leave the area. If you are cut off from your vehicle, find the quickest route to a road that is in the opposite direction of the fire and seek help.

If you cannot escape the fire, find shelter and signal for help (see "Signaling for help" later in this chapter). To buy yourself more time, cross to the other side of a natural fire break, such as a road or a river. A rock field or a lake where there is no vegetation is a good place to go as well, for smoke levels will be lower there. Also, cross ridges that are opposite of the fire. The more ridgelines you can place between you and the fire, the better.

If there's no way to escape flames – and be forewarned that forest fires can move faster than you can run – lie face down on the barest patch of ground you can find and cover

The more ridgelines you can place between you and a forest fire, the better. The smoke rising from this fire – on the first day of the Station Fire in the Angeles National Forest – was about 14 miles away, but even at that dis-tance ash fell to the ground and the sky began to turn hazy within an hour.

yourself with soil. Put your mouth to the soil, breathing through it rather than your nostrils or the air.

Lost in the wilds

> *"We're not lost, we're just misplaced."* – The Man with the Yellow Hat, *"Curious George"*

You can avoid getting lost simply by staying on the trail. Check your map frequently to make sure you're on the right trail. Keep in mind specific landmarks that you will see, and upon coming to them, look at the map to note your location and progress. Always check your map when coming to forks or adjoining trails.

Don't take shortcuts because they usually aren't. The reason a trail seems to take the long way around is because the "short" way would go through a swamp or across a steep slope. If you take a shortcut, you'll often have to take a detour, and that almost guarantees you'll get lost.

When an individual child is lost

Children can easily get lost when they wander off the trail or get out of sight of an adult.

You can avoid losing a child by always staying in visual contact of one another. Don't let children run off too far ahead, lag behind, or go off trail (that's why it's generally not advisable to play "Hide and Seek" on the trail). Children who set the pace in the lead should stop whenever they turn around and can't see an adult (and they should turn around regularly). Teach kids to stay on the trail by learning how to follow the path: recognizing blazes, rock cairns, visual clues like logs, brush piles blocking reroutes, and so on. You also can use the buddy system. One child likely will encourage the other to not wander off, and if he doesn't at least they won't be lost alone, which can be far more frightening and dangerous.

When a child realizes he's lost, he should stop, remain where he is, stay on the trail, and blow the safety whistle three times. This will help you identify your child's location sooner. Also, teach children the importance of not crying wolf. They should use the whistle only if they really are lost.

Lost children who see other hikers should tell them so. The adult hikers may know your whereabouts and be able to bring the child back to you. At the very least, the child is in care of an adult rather than alone. In this day and age, there always is fear that a stranger may be a dangerous weirdo, but on a remote trail traversed only by hikers, the odds really are against it.

Unless there are recent reports of a kidnapper or molester on the trail (in which case, you ought not to be on it anyway), the child shouldn't pass on the opportunity of receiving help as another adult might not be along for a very long time.

Likewise, children should be told that they need to answer the calls of their searchers. Some young children will not respond because they think they shouldn't talk to strangers or because they're afraid they'll be in trouble when found.

Search strategies for parents

The first thing to remember is don't panic. By keeping a cool head, you'll be able to make the best decisions about finding your children. The odds favor them being very nearby, and if they stopped walking once they realized they were lost and blow on their safety whistles, you'll find them very quickly.

Begin the search by blowing on your whistle to let the child know you're nearby. The whistle's sound will travel farther than your voice. Hopefully they will whistle back, and then you can go to them.

If the children do not respond, contact officials immediately. Even though you may find your children shortly thereafter, they may be injured and need medical attention. With a rescue team on the way, your injured children will receive help sooner.

Then begin a circular search of the immediate area, walking in a spiral pattern from a central point, known as "home." Always search in teams, and never send young children to conduct a search. Make sure some of the party stays at "home" so more of you don't become lost. Have the party at home shout the lost children's names, and if darkness falls, keep a light shining there.

Pay close attention to bodies of water such as streams and lakes. Children often are attracted to bodies of water and simply may have wandered off to take a look.

When rescuers arrive, work with them. Don't withhold any information and do as they ask. They have a lot of experience at rescue work and really are using the best strategies to quickly find your children.

You should know what your children were wearing so you can provide good descriptions of them to rescuers.

Also, always keep one of the child's belongings, such as a recently worn shirt, in your vehicle. Search dogs can use this to get the scent of the child. Some parents even take pictures of the kids' boot soles so they'll be easier to locate during a search.

When the group is lost

How do you know you're lost? When you don't know where you are *and* you don't know which way to go. The two are not mutually exclusive. You could be hiking along a trail and not be able to pinpoint on a map exactly where you are yet still be confident that you're heading in the right direction simply because no other trails have branched off yours and because key landmarks are easily identifiable on the horizon.

As soon as you're uncertain where you are and whether or not you're heading in the right direction, stop walking. It's time to figure out where you are.

As when searching for someone lost, don't panic. It's the greatest danger to anyone who is lost. Just take a rest stop and pull out your maps. Check the topo map and see if you can spot any obvious landmarks. These could include prominent peaks, roads, water towers, power lines or waterways.

If you can't locate an obvious landmark, consider tracing your way back to the last spot you checked your map and knew you were going in the right direction. From there, either head in the correct direction or return to your vehicle before you get lost again.

Should you see other hikers, don't hesitate to tell them you're lost. They'll probably be able to help you find your bearings. At the very least, they can take you to a trailhead and then hopefully back to your vehicle.

If lost, you're probably not too far away from your trail. Experienced hikers know the odds are good that they can get back to the trail:

> *"Estimate how much time has passed since you last knew where you were, then estimate how far you probably can walk in that amount of time. If you cover a mile every half hour, and 15 minutes have passed since you last saw a landmark that you knew was on your trail, at worse you're only a half-mile off course. By knowing the compass direction of a landmark you can identify, you can estimate which direction the trail is."* – Melissa F., Moab, Utah

Fair warning, though: It's probably not a good idea to go back to the trail but best to stay where you are and take comfort in knowing that you'll be fairly easy for rescuers to find. If you keep walking in the wrong direction, you likely will increase the time rescuers need to locate you.

Should you rescue yourself while a search operation is underway, be sure to let a park ranger or the authorities know. There's no need to continue the search once you're safe. Such operations are expensive and you may needlessly be draining manpower and resources away from another rescue.

Forced to stay the night

If you are lost or a member of your party suffers a serious injury, you may be forced to stay the night in the wilds. When that occurs, you must go into survival mode. But there's no need to panic. In fact, if you keep a calm head, you'll likely get out of it just fine, albeit a little tired and famished. After all, if you prepared properly, you've left plenty of clues about where you are, so a rescue crew will be there in a day or two at worse.

What you should do first when forced to stay the night depends on the situation. Shelter is primary if the weather is rainy or windy. If the day is clear and darkness is setting in, building a fire takes precedence.

If a number of you are in the party, you can split duties. As some begin building a shelter, others can gather lots of dry fuel, such as tinder, bark and small branches, for starting a campfire. Once done with this, begin conserving your energy.

In addition, take care not to get wet and stay out of the wind so you do not get chilled.

Building a shelter

Before building a shelter, you must choose a site for it. Look for dry, level ground, especially one with a natural wind break like trees or the side of a hill. Avoid dirt full of rocks and gravel and don't camp in low spots like a dry wash or depression where water might collect. Don't set up a shelter under a tree from which limbs might fall or a lone tree in a windspent field, or along a hill or a cliff in which rocks might roll down onto you. Valley floors aren't great spots either as cool air sinks to the terrain's lowest spots. Mountain ridges and passes also are poor choices as they are windy. Lightning tends to strike ridgelines as well.

To build a makeshift shelter, string a tarpaulin on a rope tied between two trees or two trekking poles; most times, you won't carry tarpaulin with you in on a day hike, of course, so you'll need to use other materials, such as a space blanket.

An emergency lean-to can be made by propping long branches against a fallen log to form a roof. Cover the branches with thinner branches that have leaves on them. You can interweave them to better keep rain off you. The thicker the layers of leaved branches, the better the protection. Garbage bags and your space blanket also can be placed as the roof in the absence of trees with leaves. Before resorting to the space blanket, though, try to find other materials nearby that could be used for the roof. If near a campground, you probably can find cardboard or even corrugated tin. The space blanket does an excellent job of keeping heat in, so it will work wonders keeping you warm at night if it stays close to your body. Likewise, don't use your rain jacket for the roof, as it will better serve you by keeping your clothes dry and warmth close to your body. Be sure to place any of the entrances of any makeshift shelter so they face away from (that is, at right angles to) the wind.

Another solution involves truly getting back to nature:
> *"Near a tree make a nest out of leaves or pine needles. An evergreen tree in a dense grove of them will do a fairly good job of keeping rain off you." – Bryan K., Missoula, Mont.*

Starting a campfire

A fire is central to keeping warm, cooking meals and feeling safe. Only build a fire if necessary, however. They can pose a great danger to children and the surrounding environment.

You'll first need to select a spot to build the fire. Begin by looking for an existing fire ring. If there isn't one (and even if there is), select a spot protected from the wind as the breeze can carry sparks from the fire. Given this, be sure that the campfire is built several feet away and downwind from your shelter. Also, don't build underneath a tree, as you don't want limbs or the roots to catch fire.

Children of all ages can help you collect the tinder, twigs and branches as they are small enough for them to carry. They'll have the best luck finding dry wood inside hollow stumps or near a tree trunks' base. Wet bark can be shaved away from dry wood and then further cut into tinder. As gathering your wood, separate it into piles by size. Keep the branches and dry brush away from the fire ring. You also may need to collect rocks for the fire pit.

Presuming there isn't a prebuilt fire ring, clear a circle of ground and place rocks at its edges. Rocks larger than your fists are best, but avoid using wet stones, especially those from a riverbed, as they can explode when heated. If you can't find any rocks, dig a trench.

Once a fire ring is made, place tinder in a small pile at its center. Tinder is the building block of your fire and can be anything that quickly ignites, such as dry grass, pine needles, paper, bark and twigs. Build a small teepee of pencil-length twigs around and over the tinder. Leave a space on one side of the teepee so you can reach the tinder with your hand. Now make another teepee, using longer and thicker sticks, but of no more than an inch thick, over the first teepee, again leaving a space in the side so you can reach your hand in. Stack a small ring of at least fist-sized stones around the teepee; this later will keep the fire from spreading to the surrounding ground and can be used as a place to stick a pot to boil water.

Remember those waterproof matches in a waterproof container and the small candle we discussed earlier? Take them out. Light the candle and place the candle beneath the tinder. This is the easiest wait to light a fire – there's no rubbing sticks together or holding magnifying glasses as shown on cable television survival shows. When the top teepee collapses in flame, you've got a good fire started and can add gradually larger branches to keep it going. As you don't want to get too large of a fire going – they can be difficult to control – keep the branches smaller than your firearm.

While kids can help build the fire ring and teepees, only an adult should start the fire. In addition, never leave a fire unattended.

Keep a bucket of water nearby, too. As you're lost, you probably don't have a bucket, so designate one of the canteens you've carried as the douse bucket. Don't use good drinking water you've carried in or water you've purified with tablets to douse the fire. Instead, carefully empty into another canteen water from the canteen that'll serve as a douse bucket. Then fill your douse canteen with local water from a stream, pond or puddle.

Don't dry anything around the fire. You'll find nylon melting, leather cracking, and wool burning. Instead, dry boots in the shade (and never over a campfire) by putting them upside down on a stick that you've pushed into the ground. Dry other equipment in the sun and wind.

When you hike out of the area the following morning or are rescued, extinguish the fire completely, dousing it in water, spreading out the coals, and smothering the burning branches and ashes with sand or dirt free of twigs and leaves. Pour on more water until each cinder is extinguished. Don't drench hot rocks with cold water, though, as the temperature change can cause an explosion. Before leaving, check the fire again to make sure nothing is burning. The pit should be cold to the touch. All of this may take a half-hour or more.

Making a bed

Place a tarpaulin or other material between you and the ground so you don't get cold or wet. Huddle together for warmth. When going to sleep, keep the flashlight next to you in case you need to get up during the night. Young children may become frightened or need to go potty, requiring you to get up. Make sure the flashlight is off or the batteries will go dead by morning.

Rationing food and water

Divide food so you can have two meals and three drinks of water for each person in the group. At dark, each person gets to eat one meal of their food ration and drink one of their water allotments. For breakfast, they can have the rest of their food ration and drink the second of their water allotments. A few hours later, they may have one more drink allotment.

Hopefully, since you've left information about when you would be back, the responsible party at home will report you as lost – and since they know which trail you were on, search parties will soon arrive before you must use local water and food sources.

Water

Using local sources of drinking water should be avoided, but sometimes you must take a calculated gamble or dehydration will set in.

The first challenge is to find a source of local water. Spring water is the best discovery, as it runs the lowest risk of being contaminated. Your next best bet is finding flowing water from a stream that is high in the mountains or hills, as it's more likely than not to be clean as it is close to its source, which is melting snow. Flowing water at the bottom of a mountain or hill is your next best choice. Still water on low-lying land is your worst.

If you're not lost but simply stuck in the wilds for a night due to an injury, check your topo map. Well-known springs often are marked on them.

In a desert, finding water at all can be nearly impossible, but it is out there if you know where to look. On seasonal waterways, the thicker and greener the vegetation the more likely the chance that you'll find standing water nearby. A grove of cottonwoods and willows almost guarantees that ground water is nearby. If there isn't any, dig in the cool sand under a willow, and you may find water only a few inches down. Puddles also may exist under large overhangs and in shaded rock crevices, particularly if they are on a hill's north side.

To collect the water, simply use one of your canteens or water bottles. Don't dump out good water that you've carried in, however, but combine it with water in another partially filled canteen. If the water source is too shallow for a canteen, spread your handkerchief across the water surface. When the handkerchief has absorbed the water, wring it out into your canteen.

Once you've collected water, you need to "clean" it before imbibing. There are three options: use water purification tablets, boil it, or use a water filter.

A variety of water purification tablets are available for sale, so follow the instructions on each packet for the best results. Generally, though, tablets have to sit in the water for at least 30 minutes – and if the water is cold, the tablets may need to mix in it overnight. Tablets always will leave a little aftertaste, ranging from iodine-like to a tart flavoring. Be aware that if you or your child has thyroid problems, water purification tablets may contain iodine and probably should not be used.

If boiling, do so for at least 5 minutes. This will kill Giardia and all but the hardiest microscopic bugs. Boiling won't remove chemical contaminates, however. In addition, if water is cloudy and you can't see any life such as fish or amphibians in it, boiling probably won't make it safe. When boiling water, do not do it in your plastic canteen or water bottle. The plastic likely will melt, or you won't be able to touch it when hot. Given this, you may want to add "cooking pot" to the list of items for your backpack, but I'd only do so if you're planning a long hike into the backcountry.

A number of water filters exist, all using different filtration systems and coming in different sizes. Whichever one you choose, make sure the filter pores are smaller than 0.2 microns. Anything larger will allow nasty bacteria to get through and remain in the water.

What are the advantages of each filter over the other? One that lacks iodine won't remove viruses, so you'll need to use water purification tablets or iodine anyway. A carbon or charcoal filter will remove chemicals that purification tablets and boiling won't get rid of. Reverse osmosis filters are best of all, removing almost everything bad and even desalinating sea water. Unfortunately, they're bulky and expensive, and you probably aren't going to carry one on a day hike let alone a camping trip.

Food

Forage for local berries before darkness sets in so you can see what you're picking. Some plants are poisonous, so familiarizing yourself with them before heading into the wilds is useful. Among common plants you should avoid are white berries and some varieties of fiddlehead. Stay away from mushrooms unless you are certain they are safe.

Other considerations

When kids need to go potty, dig catholes downwind from the campfire and from where you'll be sleeping.

Signaling for help

While you should stay put and let help come to you if lost, that doesn't mean you can't assist those looking for you.

Have someone in your party signal help by blowing three blasts on a whistle every minute or so. Hopefully, someone will find you and be able to help you out. You also can use the whistle to spell S.O.S., which is three short whistles, three long whistles, then three short whistles.

Consider building a signal fire as well. In the morning once warm, place green brush and damp bark or moss over your campfire so that it sends up a thick column of black smoke, which will attract rangers and other hikers. Make two additional fire rings so that you have three columns of black smoke rising, which signals "help."

A mirror also can be used to attract attention. Point it at the sun and then move it back and forth so that light is reflected off it. Use this method if an aircraft is passing overhead.

Displaying orange gear, especially in groups of three, signals passing hikers and rescuers that you need help.

Ground signals – giant letters made from rock, branches or your gear – can be made in open areas to let passing aircraft know you're in trouble. "I" means you have an injury, and "F" means you need food and water.

Postscript: After the Hike

> *"Let children walk with Nature, let them see the beautiful blendings and communions of death and life, their joyous inseparable unity, as taught in woods and meadows, plains and mountains and streams of our blessed star, and they will learn that death is stingless indeed, and as beautiful as life."* – John Muir

Once you've completed your first hike, pat yourself on the back. You've done a lot of work but have taken the first step into a larger world for both you and your children.

Before getting home, you may want to celebrate. Perhaps boost everyone's energy with a stop at a restaurant or somewhere else special back in civilization:

> *"After being hauled around all day in a baby carrier, my infant and toddler always enjoyed a stop at a playground near the trailhead, especially when it was in a village or park that we'd never been to before."* – Monica S., Manchester, N.H.

Such activities make a memorable end to a day hike. To keep kid's enthusiasm charged, "review" the hike in kid-friendly ways. While you really can't do this with infants, most toddlers and older kids will enjoy it.

AFTER THE HIKE

Looking at pictures of the hike once you've returned home is a fun way to remember the highlights of the trip – and to get children excited about the next adventure.

Look at your photos

Make sure you've taken photos of each kid and of the best sights you saw. For toddlers, looking at the photos may be all that you do. With older kids, you might play "Where were we?" and see if the kids can guess at what point of the trail you were on using a map. The photos can be made into posters for your family or living rooms, or you can make them into cards sent during the winter holidays.

Look at the maps

Review the map, pointing out the trail you took and where various fun things occurred or interesting sights were seen:

"Here's where we forded the stream"; "Here's where we saw the eagles"; "Here's where we skimmed rocks into the pond."

High point, low point

Ask your kids what were the highlights and the boring parts or disappointments during the hike. You may be surprised by what they say. It'll also help you make the next hike even better.

Share your hike

Have teenagers post pictures on an online photo album or maybe create a blog about your hike. Just as you researched your hike by going online and seeing what others had to say about their adventure, so others also can learn from your treks.

Get involved

If your children really enjoy hiking, they might like to attend local slide shows, lectures or orienteering courses, usually offered by sporting goods outlets, libraries and bookstores.

They also might like to meet other kids who also are into it by joining hiking or scouting clubs in your community. Many such clubs organize group hikes. Most also volunteer their time to improving trails in the parks and wilderness areas where they hike or give back in other ways, such as picking up trash along trails, clearing growth from them, or raising money for facilities and amenities like nature centers.

Go back

Revisit trails your kids really enjoyed, especially if they ask to go back there. The place is special to them and certain to become a fond memory of childhood. For many adults, revisiting a trail may seem dull, especially given that there are tens of thousands of other ones yet to explore, so to break the monotony, visit the trail in a different season.

Save the trail maps

Write on the map the day you hiked the trail and store them away in a notebook or file folder. Years from now, your kids may wish to make the same hike again ... perhaps with their own children.

Index

A

Activities and games, 132, 136, 139-153
  ABCs, 145
  Bark rubbings, 146
  Be the animal, 147
  Birdwatching, 150
  Butterfly net, 142
  Chain story, 152
  Cloud pictures, 151
  Conversation, 153
  Counting, 142
  Drawing, 149
  Finding patterns, 143
  Find your way back, 152
  Geocaching, 148
  Grab bag, 143, 144
  Hide and seek, 204
  Identify animals, 147
  Identify tracks, 148
  Identify trees and plants, 147
  I Spy, 140
  Journaling, 149
  Magnifying glass, 140
  Memory, 143
  Nature bingo, 141, 143-144
  Nature-related, 140-150
  One hundred steps, 151
  Orienteering, 148-149
  Picture hunt, 149
  Poetry on the go, 153
  Rainbows, 142
  Red light, green light, 150-151
  Rock climbing, 150
  Rock hopping, 151-152
  Scavenger hunt, 140-141, 144
  Senses, 146
  Signs of wildlife, 146
  Simon says, 151
  Sing songs, 151
  Sniff it, 144
  Sound map, 148
  Spelling bee, 152
  Tape collection, 141-142
  Treehugger, 149
  Twenty questions, 152
  "When you hear" train, 144
  Whichever way the wind blows, 147
Adhesive bandage, 88, 90, 157-158, 169, 185
Adventure Pass, 19
Alcohol, 86
Aloe vera, 88, 159-160
Altimeter, 75-76, 91
Anesthetic, 88, 189
Animals, 182-196
  Bites, 144, 183-186, 196
  Feeding, 182, 191

INDEX

Fending off, 63, 182-194
  Newborns, 195
  Rabies, 194-196
  Trapped, 196
Ants, 191
Antacid, 88
Antibacterial ointment (aka antibiotic ointment), 88, 169
Anti-diarrheal tablets, 88
Antihistamine, see *Liquid antihistamine*
Anti-itch cream, 88, 185, 187
Antiseptic, 88, 169, 182, 188
Aspirin, 88, 190

B

Baby carriers, 26, 51-57, 98, 111, 121-122, 130, 139, 155, 218
  Extras, 52-54
  Front pack, 51
Backpacks, 57-62, 66, 82, 89, 98, 102-104, 111, 151, 170, 197
  Adult packs, 58-59
  Alternatives to, 62
  How much can children carry, 60-62
  Kid's packs (aka daypacks), 59-62, 110-111, 128
Baking soda, 88, 180
Bandana, 97, 143, 152, 187
Barometer, 75-76, 91
Bathing suits, 98, 162
Batteries, 67, 76, 95, 103, 213
Beaches, 19, 23, 122

Bears, 30, 182, 191-193, 196
Bed, emergency, 213
Bees, 186
Binoculars, 96, 150
Bison, 194-195
Blisters, see *Injuries*
BLM land, 20
Bonding 6-7
Boot prints, 113-114
Breakable ice packs, 88, 169, 170
Buildings, abandoned, 118
Burrs, 182
Butterfly net, 142
Buying gear, 51-52, 59-60, 70
  Military surplus, 70
  Off-season, 70

C

Caffeinated beverages, 86
Calamine lotion, 88, 191
Camera, 66-67, 98, 103, 149
Camping, 37, 67, 69
Candle, 94, 103, 212
Canteens, 62-63, 102-103, 105, 163, 212, 214-215
  Hydration system, 63, 102
Carabiners, 66, 103, 150
Cathole, 95, 130-131, 216
Caves, 118, 197
Character, developing 9
Chiggers, 188-189
Children
  Being flexible with, 14
  Boredom, 131-132, 139, 145
  Criticizing, 15, 131, 133
  Dawdling, 128

[223]

Dirty, getting, 134
Distances they can walk, 24-27
Fear of wilds, 137-138, 213
Misbehaving, 127-138
Modifying hiking goals, 12-13
Noisiness, 134
Patience with, 14-15
Reluctant, 34-36, 135-136
Risk-taking, 134-135
Sibling rivalry, 133
Slow moving, 127-128
Tantrums, 132-133
Tiredness, 131, 138
Whining, 131
Clubs, 220-221
Coastline, 19, 23, 200
Collecting, 20, 117
Compass, 75-77, 91-92, 103, 135, 148-149
  Declination, 77
  Field interference, 77
  Grid north, 77
  Magnetic north, 77
  Protractor compass, 77
Compress, see *Gauze compress*
Cotton swab, 88, 169
Cougars, see *Mountain lions*
County parks, 19
Coyote, 182, 194-195
Crossing terrain, 121-123
  Rock hopping, 123, 151-152
  Scree, 122
  Slopes, 121-122, 127

Waterways, 122-123, 127-128

D

Deer, 182, 194-195
Dehydration, see *Injuries*
Deserts, 22, 23, 46, 124, 214
Diapers, 94-95, 103, 130, 162, 184
Disposable syringe, 89, 169
Dogs, 62, 99-100, 119
Drowning, 175-176
  Rescuing, 175-176

E

Electrolyte additives, see *Sports drinks*
Elevation gains, 27
Elk, 194-195
Emergency information sheet, 107-109
Energy pills, 86
Epipen, 89
Exercise, 8-9

F

Fanny pack, 57-58, 66, 89, 102-104, 111
Fence, 121, 146
Field guide, 78, 147, 148
Fingernail clippers, 89
Fire, 75, 94, 199, 209-213
  Building, 211-212
  Campfire, 94, 210-213, 216
  Douse bucket, 212
  Drying gear over, 212
  Emergency, 75, 210-213
  Extinguishing, 212-214

INDEX

Fire ring, 211, 217
Tinder, 94, 199, 209, 211-212
First aid, 88-90, 98, 154-191
   Animals, 182-191
   Cardiopulmonary resuscitation, 176-177
   Plants, 178-182
   Rescue breathing technique, 177
   Treating injuries, see *Injuries*
First-aid blanket, see *Space blanket*
First-aid kit, 87-90, 103-105
Flashflood, 122, 198. 201
Flashlight, 95, 103, 213
Flowers, 28. 34, 116-117
   Picking, 116-117
Food, 79, 82-86, 162, 213 216
   Berries, 116-117, 180-181, 192, 216
   Eating something you shouldn't, 165-166, 180-181
   Fiddlehead, 216
   Leftovers, 86
   Mushrooms, 181, 216
   Picnic lunch, 82, 85-86, 103
   Rationing, 213
   Snacks, 79, 103-105, 135
   Trail mix, 82-84, 111
Footwear, 40-43
   Boots, 40-43, 157, 169, 189, 207
   Sandals, 42
   Shoes, 40-41, 128, 187
   Socks, 43, 157
Forest fires, 32, 201-203
Forests, 23
Fossils, 20
   Collecting, 20
   Trails, 20
Fox, 182, 195

G
Gates, 120
Gauze bandage (aka gauze dressing), 89, 169-172, 175
Gauze compress (aka compression bandage), 89, 180, 184, 189-190
Gems, 20, 117
Gnats, 191
Gorp, see *Food*
GPS (Global Positioning System), 33, 71, 75-76, 91, 103, 200
Guidebook, 26, 34, 78

H
Handkerchief, 81, 97, 152, 159, 170-171, 214-215
Hand sanitizer, 89
Headgear, 46, 55, 66, 110, 158, 162, 187
High altitude, see *Mountains*
Hiker's safety form, 33, 107, 109-110
Hiking
   Benefits of, 6-11
   Lifelong activity, 10
   Websites, 17
Hiking partners, 137-138, 204

Hiking sticks, see *Trekking poles*
Homemade gear, 68-70
  Trekking pole, 68
  Utility belt pockets, 68-69
  Water bottle holder, 69
Hornets, 186
Horseflies, 191
Hypothermia, 46, 130, 157, 161-163

I
Illness, 156
Injuries, 154-177, 201, 206, 214
  Altitude sickness, 173
  Bleeding, 172
  Blisters, 41, 43, 93, 157-158, 178-179
  Broken bone, 171-172
  Bruise, 157, 168-169, 170-171
  Cut, 93, 157, 169, 172
  Dehydration, 157-158, 163, 173, 214
  Dislocation, 171
  Fall, 138, 157, 167, 171-172
  Fracture, 168, 170
  Frostbite, 157, 173-174, 199
  Heat exhaustion, 160-161
  Heat stroke, 160-161, 170
  Hypothermia, 170, 199-200
  Insect bite and sting, see *Insects*
  Muscle cramp, 167
  Nosebleed, 166-167
  Shock, 170, 172, 176, 181, 184
  Splinter, 166
  Sprain, 169-170
  Strain, 169-170
  Sunburn, 158-159
  Sunstroke, 157-158
  Swelling, 170-171
  Unconsciousness, 176-177
  Wind burn, 159-160
  Wounds, 169
Insects, 184-191
  Bites, 184-191
  Stings, 184-191
Insect repellent, 93, 103, 110, 169, 185-186, 189
  Applying, 185
  DEET, 93, 185
  Oil of lemon eucalyptus, 185
  Picaridin, 185
Inviting friends, 36, 132, 135

J
Jeans, 44, 162
Journal, 96-97, 149-150

K
Knife, 65-66, 68, 87

L
Lanyard, 77, 96, 103
Layering, 44-45, 162
Leave no trace, 116-117
"Leaves of three, let it be", 179
Lip balm, 92, 103, 110, 159

INDEX

Liquid antihistamine, 89, 191
Litter, 117-118
    Burying, 118
Livestock, 196
Lost, 90, 92, 97, 105, 112, 114, 118, 128, 201, 204-208
    Finding lost child, 205-207
    Finding way back, 207-208
    What lost child should do, 205
Lyme disease, 187-188

M

Magnifying glasses, 96, 140, 142, 212
Maps, 32-33, 71-75, 77, 94, 102-104, 111, 123, 135, 204, 207, 214, 219, 221
    Guides, printed, 72-74
    Handmade, 72-73
    Map cases, 75
    Orienting, 77
    Road, 72-74
    Satellite photo, 74
    Software, mapping, 74
    Topographical map, 33, 72-74, 112, 149, 207, 214
    USGS topo maps, 73-74
Marshland, 123, 184
Matches, 94, 103, 212
Meadow, 120
Medical tape, 89
Milk, 80-82, 104
    Bottle, 81-82, 104
Mines, 118, 168

Mittens, 44, 48, 174
Mobile phone, 90-91, 98, 103, 106, 111, 120, 177
Moisturizer, 89, 160
Mole skin, 89, 158
Moose, 194-195
Mosquitoes, 187
Mountain lions, 193-196
Mountains, 22-23, 27, 31, 46, 122, 124, 158, 163, 173, 184, 197-201, 214
Multi-purpose tool, 65, 87, 89, 103
Muscle cramps, 164, 167

N

National forests, 17, 19, 100, 106, 114, 124, 202-203
National parks, 18, 100, 124, 182, 202
National Parks and Federal Recreational Lands Pass, 18
Nature, communing with, 7-8, 132
Nature-deficit disorder, 7
Navigational tools, 71-78, 96
No-see-ums, 191

O

Off-trail hiking, 118
Orienteering, 148-149, 220

P

Pacifier, 82, 104
Packing, 102-105, 135
Pack out what you pack in, 86, 117-118
Pain reliever (aka aspirin), 89

Parking, 105-106, 112-113,
Peakbagging, 27, 173, 201
Pedometer, 149
Pens, 96-97
Plants, 178-182
Pocket mirror, 97, 217
Poison ivy, 112, 178-180
  Cream, 89, 179-180
  Soap, 89, 180
Poison oak, 112, 178-180
Poison sumac, 112, 178-180
Potty, going, 130-131, 213, 216
  Fear, 131
Prescriptions, 92, 103
Private property, 21, 117, 120, 196

R
Raccoon, 195
Rain, 24, 197-198
Poncho, 103, 198
Rain gear, 48, 103
Rain jacket, 44, 48, 103-104
Re-sealable plastic bags, 20, 75, 82, 90, 93-95, 97, 103, 130
Rest stops, 14, 31, 75, 128, 134, 147-148, 152, 161-162, 167, 207
Rockhounding, 20, 35
Rocky Mountain spotted fever, 187-188
Rope, 66-67, 103, 209
Ruins, 117
Running ahead, 114, 128-130

S
Safety whistle, 93, 103-105, 134, 206
Satellite photos, 33, 112
Scorpions, 190
Shelter, emergency, 63, 67, 209-210
Sherpa, 62
Shorts, 43
Signal for help, 202, 216-217
  Displaying orange gear, 217
  Fire rings, 217
  Ground signals, 217
  Mirror, 217
  Signal fire, 217
  S.O.S., 216-217
  Whistle, 216-217
Significant other, 136-137
Skills, developing, 9-10
Skunks, 194-195
  Getting rid of smell, 194
Sling, 89, 171-172
Smash-and-runs, 106-107
Snakes, 112, 114, 123, 183-184
Snakebite kit, 89, 183
Soda, 86
Space blanket, 93-94, 97, 103, 162, 210, 217
Spade, 95
Spiders, 189-190
Sports drinks, 80, 89, 165
State parks, 18
Stinging nettles, 180
Stroller, 57
Sunglasses, 46-47, 55, 110, 159
Sunscreen, 55, 92, 103-104,

159
 Applying, 110, 159
 PABA, 92
Survival mode, 208-209
Swimming, 136

T
Tarpaulin, 98, 103, 170, 209, 213
Teething ointment, 89
Thermometer, 89
Thorns, 182
Ticks, 187-188
Tissue paper, 97
Toilet paper, 93, 95, 103-104, 130-131
Toilet trowel, 95, 103
Tourniquet, 172
Towels, 98
Trail
 Etiquette, 118-121
 Length, 24-27
 Mapping out, 32-33
 Midpoint payoff, 28-29
 Overgrown, 28
 Quality, 27-28
 Rules of, 115-121, 127
 Safety, 111-112, 134-135
 Selecting a destination, 16-34
 Switchbacks, 118-119
 Uniqueness, 28-29
 Width, 27-28
Trailhead, 33, 78, 99, 101-102, 105, 112-115, 124, 136, 207, 218
Trail markers, 120, 123-125
 Blazes, 124-125, 204
 Cairns, 120, 124, 204

INDEX

Directional signs, 124
 Flags, 125
 Signposts, 124
Trail mix, see *Food*
Trail register, 106
Travel time, 31-32, 75
Trekking poles, 63-66, 68, 110-111, 121-123, 176, 209
Telescopic pole, 64
Tips, 63-64
Turf, 27
Turn-back time, 33, 125-126
Tweezers, 87, 89, 166, 182, 186

V
Videocamera, 98

W
Walking poles, see *Trekking poles*
Walking sticks, see *Trekking poles*
Wasps, 186
Water, drinking, 33, 62-63, 79-80, 87, 103, 112, 163, 167, 212-216
 Bad water, 165-166
 Boiling, 165, 215-216
 Filtering, 165, 215-216
 Giardia lamblia, 165
 Local sources, 80, 165, 214
 Purification tablets, 89, 165, 212, 215-216
 Rationing, 213
Waterproof bags, 66, 75
Water safety, 175-176

[229]

Weather, 22-24, 197-200
   Flashflood, 198, 201
   Fog, 126, 200
   Lightning, 197-198, 209
   Rain, 197-198, 209
   Snowstorm, 199-200
   Thunderstorm, 126, 197-199
   Tornado, 199
   Weather blanket, see *Space blanket*
Wells, 168
West Nile virus, 187
Wet wipes, 93, 95, 97, 104, 130-131
Wildflower displays, 24
Wilderness changing, 10-11
Wildlife sanctuaries and refuges, 21
Windbreaker, 44
Winter hiking, 22-23, 42, 45, 48, 69-70, 173-175
   Gear, 69-70
Wolves, 194
Wounds, 169
Wristwatch, 91-92, 104
   Compass, use as, 91-92
   Digital, 91

Y

Yellowjackets, 186

About the Author

Rob Bignell is a long-time hiker, journalist, and author of the popular "Hikes with Tykes," "Headin' to the Cabin," and "Hittin' the Trail" guidebooks and several other titles. He and his son Kieran have been hiking together for the past eight years. Before Kieran, Rob served as an infantryman in the Army National Guard and taught middle school students in New Mexico and Wisconsin. His newspaper work has won several national and state journalism awards, from editorial writing to sports reporting. In 2001, The Prescott Journal, which he served as managing editor of, was named Wisconsin's Weekly Newspaper of the Year. Rob and Kieran live in Hudson, Wis.

CHECK OUT THESE OTHER HIKING BOOKS BY ROB BIGNELL

"Headin' to the Cabin" series:
- Day Hiking Trails of Northeast Minnesota
- Day Hiking Trails of Northwest Wisconsin

"Hikes with Tykes" series:
- Hikes with Tykes: Games and Activities

"Hittin' the Trail" series:
Minnesota
- Interstate State Park (ebook only)

Wisconsin
- Barron County
- Bayfield County
- Burnett County (ebook only)
- Chippewa Valley
- Crex Meadows Wildlife Area (ebook only)
- Douglas County
- Interstate State Park (ebook only)
- Polk County (ebook only)
- Sawyer County

National parks
- Best Sights to See at America's National Parks
- Grand Canyon (ebook only)

ORDER THEM ONLINE AT:
hikeswithtykes.com/hittinthetrail_home.html

www.ingramcontent.com/pod-product-compliance
Lightning Source LLC
Chambersburg PA
CBHW061429040426
42450CB00007B/964